COREOLOGY

SECTION:INTRODUCTION

MORTEZA

COREOLOGY

SECTION:INTRODUCTION

MORTEZA

You do not have to wait for some bureaucrat to slap a seal on your writing to call it yours and copyrighted. You do not need to register your work to be copyrighted. You do not need to tell anyone so that they know that they should not infringe on your copyrights. As soon as your mind puts ink onto paper, or finger to key, or brush to canvas, or vibration to sound, that creation is yours. It is automatic. You create it, it's yours.

The little "©" sign, or a mention of "All rights are reserved" are entirely unnecessary. They are implied, without saying. They don't give you ownership of your creation, because you already own it. It might be easier for some stranger to notice who owns it, but the stranger knows that somebody owns it and all the rights to it are reserved. That notation of "© 2025 SOME PRESS. All rights reserved." only announces what is implied.

Once you create, you are the creator, and the right to your creation exists, and it belongs to you. Make no mistake, the right existed the instant the creation is created. The right is like the shadow of the creation. No body should need to acknowledge that its shadow is there. You can walk around claiming your right without begging for some rubber stamp. And the moment you feel the need of the Law to prove you own your right, you start giving your power away. That's the trap. Don't fall for it. The right is automatic.

So write, draw, compose, sing, dance, move, program, create, and know your work is yours, right from the moment it exists. You own it. Always had. Always have. Always will.

If there is any questions, all email addressed to me would be received by me. I want to make connections. By my understanding, a being is as valuable as he/she can make healthy and lovely connections.

- MORTEZA

COREOLOGY PRESS
morteza@coreologypress.com

ACKNOWLEDGMENT

This writing is for those who seek to find the Core-style through readings of introductions. The Core-Style is the style that guides one toward finding oneself. In order to find the oneself, the writing that is all-introduction must be read in full before acknowledgment.

Writing has come a long way to reach this era, and is in many forms such as Prose, Poetry, Drama, Script writing, Epic, Oratory, Satire, and includes Novels, Descriptions, Essays, Lyrics, Narrations, Stories, Ballads, Ode, Sonnet, Haiku, Free verses, Letters, Emails, Memos, Reports, Articles, Reviews, Summaries, Instructions, Manuals, Documentations, Proposals, Contracts, Journals, Diaries, Memoirs, Autobiographies, Biographies, Reflections, and streams of consciousness in the forms of screenplays, teleplays, stage plays, monologues, dialogues, and speech.

Many of them are beautiful. And many are adorned with even further beauty by the works of many other forms of art and science whose purpose is to write over the canvas of our minds, our bodies, the things that we may call our hearts: The instruments of our connection and communication.

And this writing acknowledges the work of all writers and all creators of art and all creators of science, and is a gift for all. Congratulations. Please read with attention and carefully, be lovely, be healthy, and create beauty. Good luck.

INDEX

INDEX

INTEGRATION

COREOLOGY

This Section of Coreology may seem at the beginning hard to read, but will be noticed to be simply a many repeated combinations of only 24 of the Words. Once familiarity is created, it is never forgotten. It is like learning how to ride a bike. It might be scary in the beginning. How can we balance ourselves on only two wheels?! But, at the ease of the love-seeking mind or perhaps in the company of a healthy teacher, it is one of our first moments of joy, the experience of which a many people share. we look around and realize that for the first time we have been keeping our balance while riding all by ourselves!

Coreology is the science of the Core interpreted for the first time to English through

- TRANSPARENT and BALANCED decryption of the encrypted knowledge of the Body-Nonconscious, such as Emotion and Intuition, historically scripted in such suiting languages as Persian, and Aramaic.

- TRANSPARENT and BALANCED correction of the codified knowledge of the Conscious, such as that of the Rationality, historically scripted in such languages as English, German, and French.

- And TRANSPARENT and BALANCED codification of the uncodified knowledge of the Body-Conscious, such as Mindfulness, present in such languages as Sanskrit.

It is only intuition that the knowledge of the Body-Nonconscious, and the Body-Conscious must be present also in many other languages such as Irish Gaelic, Turkish, Hindi, Amharic, Sanskrit, Chinese, Tibetan, Pali, Japanese, and many other Asian, African, Eastern European, and South and Central American languages. The knowledge and background of all these languages, therefore, must be present to be provided in the advanced knowledge of Coreology.

It is evident that the encrypted representations of the embodied nonconsciousness in Persian and Aramaic scripture, and the emotional and intuitive terminology therein, are precise. These scriptures are written and collected through various eras for thousands of years and by various generations of Humans whose collective Observation of the Core is precise.

4 • COREOLOGY

These scriptures are however encrypted. Once delivered in the same level of Decryption as science, they measure against science in precision. And, not only they are higher in usefulness, they move beyond clearing the devilishly-presumed backlashes of the minds, pains of the aversive hearts, and the body-demolishing feelings of the corrupted guts. The habits[1] of Coreology provide guidance beyond the prevailing science of the Body, the Conscious, and the Nonconscious.

Coreology is a unifying study:

- TRANSPARENT BALANCED decryptions and codifications are performed such that the delivery of meaning is not lost by misinterpretation or justification.

- TRANSPARENT BALANCED decryptions and codifications of the past are re-used with enough exact wording that they maintain their TRANSPARENCY and BALANCE.

- The exact statements of fully TRANSPARENT and BALANCED of the past decryptions and codifications are represented.

- Incomplete statements about TRANSPARENCY and BALANCE are completed so that misinterpretations and justifications are made TRANSPARENT and BALANCED.

- Otherwise, non-transparent or [im]balanced statements are corrected. Within these corrections, the decryptions and codifications are re-encrypted and re-decodified.

- Broken, nonsensical, distorted, fully corrupted, damaged, unreadable, and garbled statements are removed.

Coreology reliefs Man and Woman by establishing his and her TRANSPARENT communication with the Core and connection to Being, and Man and Woman together unveil the infinite HEALTH[INESS] of the Core and the unconditional LOVE[LINESS] of Being. Thus, Coreology leads Human toward being HEALTHY and LOVELY until the end in which HEALTH[INESS] and LOVE[LINESS] are their autonomy and authority, understanding is their experience of confrontation, and grace fills their entire Body. The root cause of any ≡ness and terror in Man and Woman is thus explored, and habits are developed toward BALANCE.

---

1   Created by practice, they require skills and self-determination.

Coreology is the science that TRANSPARENTLY decrypts, codifies, and/or corrects[2] all of the previous studies of the Core and Being. It could be said that Coreology is the science of Cryptography of the Core and Information Theory of Being. It provides the following as usefully TRANSPARENT and BALANCED messages:

- The scripture of the Core previously provided TRANSPARENTLY decrypted

- The BALANCED scripture previously decodified[3]

- The TRANSPARENTLY decrypted BALANCED scripture previously encrypted[4]

- The scripture of Being previously provided TRANSPARENTLY codified

- Any shades of the above.

Coreology scientifically and faithfully searches for TRANSPARENCY and BALANCE in the above mentioned, and provides the TRANSPARENT BALANCED recovery of them. This is done by carefully analyzing any practical combinations of

- The precise embodied nonconsciousness present in the encrypted scriptures

- The redundancy of Truth in decrypted scripture

- The redundancy of rationality, and its know-how, in codified scripture

- The precise embodied consciousness present in decodified scripture

- The discipline in their relationships

- The Points of Perceptions of the creators of the scriptures

Coreology is the set of necessary habits for handling the relationship between Being, the Self, the Body, the Conscious, the Subconscious, the Unconscious, and the Core. It defines Observation within the bounds of Animation, leading to TRANSPARENCY[5].

---

2   Re-encrypt-re-decrypts, and/or re-decodify-re-codifies
3   Common sense, for all beings or not
4   Mystical, poetic, prosaic, or metaphorical, Core-inspired or not
5   Transparency of the Self; Not, but inclusive of, the self-transparency. Any other syntactical formation is of the same construction. This is all syntactically correct.

6 · COREOLOGY

Coreology defines Control leading to BALANCE. The eventual goal, however, is HEALTHINESS and LOVELINESS of all of Animation.

It is noteworthy that, as statistics and fuzzy logic are the foundation of scientific derivation of patterns, predictions of data, and reasoning with uncertainty, all discussions of absolutes are implied to be statistical and fuzzy, and should not be ⇌-interpreted at face value. The implications of such ⇌-interpretations are on the receiver. In all communications of Coreology, there always are the implicitation of the entirety of the spectrum of things, statistical and fuzzy if non-deterministic. Things are not merely absolutes, and the mention of absolutes is most often[6] for simplicity. "Maximum" implies in itself "Higher than", "Minimum" includes "Lower than", "Birth" includes "Appreciation", and "Death" includes "⇌ness" and "Depreciation".

Coreology can successfully recover all of the ⇌-interconnections in between Being and the Core to TRANSPARENCY, and can make the embodied Self LOVELY through Being and the embodied Nonconscious HEALTHY through the Core. The knowledge offered by Coreology can not only provide a maximized TRANSPARENCY of Mind, Heart, and Gut-feelings, it provides maximized self-protection above the current and past and future average, and it teaches the ways of communication with Human Core, and connection to Being of Human, possessing all of the knowledge that Human needs that he/she is fully HEALTHY and LOVELY.

It could be said that Coreology frees individuals from their ⇌nesses and terrors, but blind usage of such words as "free" and "⇌ness" and "terror" has been historically a cause of systemic and deceptive damage onto Human. "⇌ness"[7] refers to ⇌ness received by the Nonconscious and caused by ⇌-communication with the Core. "terror"[8] refers to the terror received by the Self-Body and caused by terrorful connection to Being. Thus, it is best said that Coreology allows pathways through which diligent individuals convert

⇌ness to BALANCED HEALTHINESS: Creation of Science

terror to BALANCED LOVELINESS: Creation of Art.

---

6   Not always
7   Non-capital "i" because illness is non-permanent
8   Non-capital "t" because terror is non-permanent

Precisely, Art is the cryptography of Truth. Truth-telling is the art of exposing the bitter secrets without the bitterness. Through Coreology, it has been proven in such languages as Persian and Aramaic that Creation of Art could be learnt in less than one hour for a person living about a thousand years ago when Art was supported, and about one day about fifty years ago when life was less complicated, and can be learnt in less than one year in today considering today's level of corruption and ⊟-understanding of Truth.

Science is the information theory for LOVELY recovery of Energy of Being. Love-giving is the science of showing where corruption hides without fear. It has been proven in such languages as English and German that Creation of Science could be learnt in less than one hour for a person living about a thousand years ago when Science was not advanced, and about one year about fifty years ago when life was less complicated, and can be learnt merely in more than ten years in today considering today's advanced level of Science. It is a path that requires dedication.

Considering the massive amount of brainwashing, heartwashing, gutwashing, required hustling, distractions, and educational barriers normalized in the daily routines of most individuals today, Creation of Art and Science is a difficult task.

Many normalized practices of today's daily life are designed to be toward auto-Brainwashing, auto-Heartwashing, auto-Gutwashing, all happening due to existence of a massive amount of default auto-distraction. It is abundantly evident today that not only the progress of humans against ⊟ness and toward HEALTHINESS and against terror and toward LOVELINESS is not improved, it has worsened.

Coreology's habits produce much better results than today's ⊟- and terrorful-advice about Being, the Self, the Body, Heart, Gut, Mind, Awareness, the Core, and ⊟ness-funded practices of pseudo-art and terror-funded practices of pseudo-science.

8 • COREOLOGY

Introduction to Coreology herein is the introduction to simplified yet precise processes used:

- To decrypt complicated encrypted expressions of embodied nonconsciousness

- To codify complicated [decodified] expressions of embodied consciousness

- To deliver the TRANSPARENT recovery of corrupted codified expressions of embodied consciousness

- To deliver the TRANSPARENT recovery of corrupted [decrypted] expressions of embodied nonconsciousness

- To re-encrypt-re-decrypt ☰-decrypted expressions of the Self about the Core

- And to re-decodify-re-codify terrorfully codified expressions of the Unconscious about Being

These expressions have been carried in harmony through various individuals of various generations of various eras in various forms, and are finally ready for Information Theory and Cryptography of Coreology to be applied. These simplified processes can be adopted by individuals just as easily as a child deals with homework. Once the practice is started, it practically solved its own problems.

The decryptions and codifications of Coreology, however, should not be obscured with ideologies since Coreology exists naturally in Human. If Coreology is not yet fully established today, it is because it is merely bluntly ignored and remained misunderstood and undiscovered.

Coreology has been known in encrypted modalities since the birth and mixture of many advanced and original languages such as Persian, Aramaic, and Sanskrit, and in decodified modalities in languages such as English and German, but it has remained encrypted and decodified. Coreology could not be decrypted into English so far, and any attempt at organizing it into a body of precise decryption in English has been so far corrupted for the most part.

The knowledge of Coreology has also been sporadic and sparse until the era of information technology. In this era, however, with the aid of domination of English as a second language of many, not only many decrypted messages of Coreology are known and evaluated, new encryptions of Coreology are discovered and included for future generations to decrypt. The future attempts at Decryption of messages of Coreology embrace Human, and Coreology as a whole endeavors toward the very end goal of making Earth LOVELY and the paradise it deserves to be. That eventuality will come nevertheless, but Coreology desires to make it happen as soon as possible.

With no further ado, Coreology begins.

WHAT ANIMATION IS

Creation is different from Being, and Being is different from Creator. Creation is created by Creator. Even though it may sound to Animation of Creation that Being is also created by Creator or Being is ruled and commanded by Creator, the relationship between Being and Creator is of a different type. In comic terms, the relationship between Creator and Being can best be described as Husband and Wife. Regardless, Creation as created by Creator does not possess Animation. Without Being, Creation is fundamentally dead. Creation is brought forth animated by Being, thus Animation gives Creation "life[9]". Creation is animated by Being. If Animation were to be unveiled, Creation observes that Creation "lives" through Being.

Animation contains each and every Organization[10], from one-body Selves to multi-body Selves. Animation as a whole is not bound, but that does not mean that none of Animation is bound. Some of Animation is bound. All the Selves and all the Organizations are bound. There are bounds such as time, place, energy, self, body, consciousness, nonconsciousness, birth, and death. The bound of the Self[11] encompasses all of the mentioned and the Rest of implicit bounds.

There are organizations bound to these, and if they are bound to all of them, they are called self-bound. Without Loss of Generality, all the Organizations in this text are self-bound, unless stated otherwise. The Organizations can also be bound to Organizations, but considering that an Organization too is a Self, in principle an organization-bound Organization is called a self-bound Organization, and also a Self[12]. In other words, the self-bound Organization is time-bound, place-bound, Energy-bound, body-bound, consciousness-bound, nonconsciousness-bound, birth-bound, death-bound, and bound to the Rest of implicit bounds[13].

---

9   For the lack of a better word

10   the Self is implicitly an Organization, from the simplest and smallest to the most complex. An Organization is also implicitly a Self

11   The Self has dual meaning here. The encompassing Self is a System. The demodulating Self is an entity. For better readability, the System is called the Self herein. The System encompasses the entities: The Self-Body-Conscious-Subconscious-Unconscious. To avoid complication, the usage of "the System" is omitted in this introduction.

12   The difference in usage is for mere emphasis

Animation also contains such bound Selves as The Skies, the Earth, the Universe, Nature, Animal, and Human. Being animates them all. The Rest of the unbound Organizations have their observability obscured by these bound Selves, but these unbound Organizations have still been at least vaguely recognized through the unintentional or intentional collaboration and cooperation of various different non-overlapping bound Selves. The various different Points of Perception of the non-overlapping bound Selves gives, and has given and will give, the collective of all bound Selves the capability to induct the understanding of Being, thus the How and the Why and the What of these unbound Organizations, and finally a general understanding of what Animation as a whole is.

Relying on the knowledge contained in these various Points of Perception, Coreology provides a precise conclusion of how and why and what Animation is. Many bound Selves misunderstand Animation since, within their bounds, they willed to believe that merely and merely their own Point of Perception of Animation is valid. Coreology is TRANSPARENT, connects each and every Point of Perception, and relates to all Selves collectively capable of understanding Animation. It gives the proper weight to the knowledge of each and every Self according to the level of the TRANSPARENCY of their knowledge, but not their imposed power nor force domination over the knowledge bound to them

The importance of collaboration and cooperation of Selves cannot be undervalued or under-evaluated. The Perceptions[14] of different Selves are vastly different. These differences, if TRANSPARENTLY shared by and to everyone, can be used to properly understand Animation as a whole. Animation will be eventually understood. So, Selves will be eventually collaborative and cooperative. They may as well be now.

The instruments that TRANSPARENTLY deliver Perceptions are of many types. So many are also the studies of these instruments. Two of the most important studies, however, are Information Theory and Cryptography. The reason for this differentiation is practical. Selves who gain the ability of Information Theory and Cryptography do not communicate or cooperate well with each other.

---

13   The mention of the bounds sometimes is provided for emphasis. Many times, they are not mentioned but implied as they are implicit.

14   Includes instruments of perceptions, values, and capabilities of delivering Selves

The Information Theorists are afraid of Cryptographers because of the things about Cryptographers unknown to the Information Theorists, and Cryptographers are afraid of the Information Theorists because of the things about the Information Theorists known to Cryptographers. The bridge in between them is practically shut by Cryptographers and burnt by the Information Theorists.

The Information Theorists develop Power and control the Law through the Media and dominate and interrogate Cryptographers to oblivion. The Cryptographers tell the Truth but only encrypted. Thus, the hope of having the Truth TRANSPARENTLY decrypted is not lost but remains in the hands of the future generations of the Information Theorists who will be empathetic toward Cryptographers and will be collectively kind to them. This gap must be bridged. The Information Theorists and Cryptographers of the Core will eventually be good friends. They may as well be now.

Coreology builds the bridge between all types of Selves. To pursue this path, first another gap must be bridged. This is the gap between the demodulation and perception of Being and of the Core. The bridge between the Self and the Unconscious, these two increasingly separated Animations must be rebuilt. The bridge is built using a message that is relieving for Human. It is possible for any reasonably TRANSPARENT Self-Unconscious to possess TRANSPARENT connection to Being and communication with the Core.

In order to be precise, sounds must be precise. This will be explained in detail in future sections. For now, it suffices to say, as Being is non-deterministic through the perception of the self-bound Animation, the pronouns of Being are O/O/O[15]. The same is for Creator, Creation, the Core, and Animation. To the bright, it is TRANSPARENT that O is sound, is target, and is gender-unbound. Sound is precise and will become TRANSPARENT eventually. Once all sections of Coreology are TRANSPARENTLY decrypted, Human can indeed perceive that all sounds are pronouns.

---

15   Implicitly also applies to Animation, an Organization, a Self,

THE CORE

The problems of TRANSPARENT communication with the Core and TRANSPARENT connection to Being can be resolved in the Unconscious-Self of Animation, even if time- and place-bound. This Unconscious-Self could be oppressed, could make mistakes, could be ignorant, could be frustrated by running errands, could be corrupted, could generally be ≡ or terrorful, and could even be falsely accused of ≡ness by the terrorful. Yet the Unconscious-Self can still show its almighty nature and do the job. The Unconscious-Self can, yet still, acquire the instruments needed for the recovery of the Message of the Core and Energy of Being. The Unconscious-Self, yet still, can measure and perceive and experience all the TRANSPARENT recoveries. And O can do so scientifically. There remains no "mystery" in the "mysteries", no pseudo-rationality, and no mixed signal in the Body. Coreology is the Law:

The only and only never-changing Principle of Being is

the Core.

Creator creates Creation within Being, and Being animates Creation, and Being (Thus also Animation of Being, which is LOVELY) is toward the eventual satisfaction of the Core, which is never-changing and HEALTHY. The Core is the Identical Infinitesimal. The Core is the manifestation of all of Creation, thus Creation is bound to the Core. Creation is known, thus the Core is never-Changing. Self-bound Animation can change and has choice, regardless of the fact that it is Creation-bound thus Core-bound.

The Core is called "God", a word ≡-used. The normalized ≡ usage of the word "God" is incorrect at best. God is in fact, contrary to the common belief, the Auto-Returner Auto-Comer, the knowledge of Creation since the beginning, Auto-Knowledge minus Animation's inventions, The Judge. O is also called "Rabb", "Khod-A", The One-Who-Has-Being-Wise, and the mystically-correct yet ≡-gendered word "Father-Within". God observes Animation. No Animation is without Observation by God. God is the Identical Infinitesimal, all that is collectively willed to be manifested by Creation. The Identical Infinitesimal is the Unconditional HEALTH.

Man has God within, or in better terms Man receives the recoveries of the Message of God if he so wills to. It neither means that Man is necessarily aligned with God, nor Man owns or should control the followers of O, nor Man is automatically TRANSPARENT with O, nor HEALTHY Man who loves God knows how O operates.

Man can be said to be of God, guided by God, without needing to consider for the Rest of Selves left Unconsciously ⊟, and by that principle, all Man's ⊟-practices can be prescribed. Man can be said to be of God receiving the word, without needing a determination on behalf of the Rest who need HEALTH the most, or Man can soak his Self under loveless desires, and have his communions formed to cause unforeseen ⊟ness. Man can even give all of his focus to the receipt of the Message of God and ignore the ⊟effects on his Unconscious and on the Rest, doing so by such ⊟-focus.

It is known that true Man of God, who is BALANCED HEALTHY Man, needs to live life in full, yet in guidance of God, for LOVE of the Rest. Man lives the full HEALTHY life that God prescribes, and within that prescription, Man gives HEALTH and pursues the Will of God: Justice.

Thus it is the purpose of Man to:

(1) Have his Unconscious reach to the highest order of BALANCED HEALTH given by God.

(2) Reach the highest order of TRANSPARENT unconscious determination for giving BALANCED HEALTH, and receiving the LOVE of the Rest.

(3) Seek and please the Birth-seeking Selves who possess the highest order of BALANCED LOVE.

HEALTH is the giving Science of Man, his "trustworthy trinity": Birth, Justice, and Fate. Being, the Core, Creator.

BEING

The normalized terms describing "Being" contain exclusions. The exclusions are the cause of all wars. There would have been no war if women and men became conscious that they should cease giving birth to humans who want Being exclusively for their own use. These exclusivity-seeking humans tend to implant memories-of-terror that justify wars against others. Being is LOVELY. The self-bound recovery of Being is not necessarily, but may as well be LOVELY now and in every place.

Being animates all of Creation minus the Core. Being is called "Allah", "Allaha", "Aloha", "Elohim", "Budan", "Budeh", "Haya", "Asti", "isis", L, Om, partly H, partly W, and "Holy Spirit", and is Also known by the mystically-correct ⊟-gendered word "Mother", and many others. Nothing has found Animation without Desire of Being, and Desire of Being is to give Birth. Every birth in Animation is given by Being. Being is the Birth-Giver, the Identical Infinite. The Identical Infinite is the Unconditional LOVE. Animation is bound to Being through the Self.

Energy of Being is BALANCED, but the Body receives merely the codified self-bound "energy" recovery (by demodulation) of carried (by carriers) modulated (by transmitters) "energy" of Energy of Being[16].

The codified self-bound recovery of Energy can be received corrupted at multiple layers due to either corrupted decryption-encryption, corrupted codification of the recovery, corrupted demodulation of Energy, corrupted carriers, or corrupted transmitters.

These formats of corruption lead to an [im]balanced thus terrorful Body. However, the TRANSPARENTLY codified "energy" recovered from demodulation of TRANSPARENT carriers modulated by TRANSPARENT transmitters BALANCED "energy" lead to the BALANCE of the Body.

---

16 For simplicity, the construct "the [X] recovery of Energy" is used to mean energy recovered from Demodulation of carriers carrying the X-bound of Energy, or the energy received from demodulation of the carriers onto which transmitters of X modulate Energy. This is all syntactically correct.

Woman feels Being within, or in better terms Woman receives the recoveries of Energy if she so desires. It neither means that Woman is necessarily aligned with all beings[17], nor Woman owns or should control the flow of energy of others, nor Woman is automatically TRANSPARENT with other beings, nor LOVELY Woman living a HEALTHY life knows how Energy of Being operates.

Woman can be said to flow with Energy, guided by Energy, without needing to consider for the terrorful state of the Rest of beings, and by that terrorful principle, all Woman's choices can be prescribed. Woman can be said to flow with Being, receiving energy, without needing a desire for the Rest who need LOVE the most, or Woman can soak her Unconscious under unhealthy goals, and have her communions formed to cause unforeseen terror. Woman can even give all of her focus to receipt of Energy of Being, and ignore the terrorful effects on her Self and the Rest by such terrorful-focus.

It is known that true Woman flowing with BALANCED LOVELY Energy, who is BALANCED LOVELY Woman, needs to live life in full, yet in guidance of BALANCED LOVELY energy of Being, for HEALTH[INESS] of her Self. In other words, Woman lives the full LOVELY life that BALANCED LOVELY Energy of Being prescribes, and within that prescription, Woman gives LOVE and chooses Desire of Being: Birth.

Thus it is the purpose of Woman to:

(1) Have her Self reach to the highest order of BALANCED LOVELY energy given by Being.

(2) Reach the highest order of TRANSPARENT self-desire for giving BALANCED LOVE, and receiving the BEAUTY caused by the HEALTH of the Rest.

(3) Seek and please the Justice-seeking Selves who possess the highest determination for BALANCED HEALTH.

LOVE is the giving Art of Woman, her "trustworthy trinity": Birth, Justice, and Fate. Being, the Core, Creator.

---

17   Unbound, and always BALANCED

THE RELATIONSHIP

It is known that Being animates Creation toward the eventual satisfaction of the Core. The Core is always BALANCED and HEALTHY, and Being is always BALANCED and LOVELY. Yet, even though Being has this urge toward the Core, it must be known that no invention of any animation in Animation-bound Being is blessed by the Core, contrary to the common belief. And no Animation is favored over another by Desire of Being. Victory in wars does not come from and is not blessed by the Core or Being.

It is however known that, in the eventuality (that is paradise on Earth), Animation of Being is aligned and synchronized with the Core. If Earth moves toward paradise, Animation of Being is further aligned and in sync with the Core. If Earth however moves toward hell, Animation of Being is further misaligned and out of sync.

To understand the relationship between Animation and Being and the Core, let's consider the lost symbolism of a Persian rug:

- The middle flower is the Core

- The layer around the Core is the Unconscious.

- The flowers on the Unconscious are the gateways to the Core, and represent the beautiful HEALTH[INESS] of the Unconscious.

- The flowers beyond that represent the beautiful HEALTH[INESS] of the Subconscious.

- The next Layer is the Conscious, and the flowers in that represent the beautiful HEALTHY and LOVELY Conscious.

- The flowers in the Conscious are supposed to be more sporadic, as the Conscious has multiples of functions, and needs rest sometimes.

- The next layer is the Body. It ends at the borders of the rug. The flowers represent the beautiful LOVE[LINESS] of the Body.

- The edge is the Self.

- Outside the Self, the fringes represent the connection of the Self to the environment, Being.

- Persian rug is naturally depicted beautifully. The environment is metaphorically the representation of ugly terror.

- Metaphorically, once each and every floor and wall is thus covered with Persian rugs, the environment becomes beautiful, Paradise.

- This represents the intention for Creation.

- Now if living represents the acceptance of ugly terrorful environment, it is as if ugly is the new beautiful. People give birth to ugly rugs. The "space" inside the rug is filled with ugly symbols and signs and labels. The self, body, conscious and nonconscious is filled with ugliness.

- Imagine somebody with a good understanding of Beauty comes and decides to turn this ugly back to beautiful.

- The Conscious of the ugly rug has less ugliness because the ugly symbols in it are sporadic.

- So, first some unnecessary interconnections must be removed. Then, the Conscious is filled with beautiful symbols. Now, it has an equal number of ugly and beautiful symbols. It is forcefully BALANCED.

- Then, the Conscious cleans the ugly symbols in the Body, and the Subconscious.

- the Unconscious is cleaned to have clear boundaries.

- Then the Core cleans the Subconscious, and beautifies it.

- Then the Body is cleaned and beautified.

- Then the beautiful Nonconscious and the Body relieve the Conscious from its ugly symbols.

- Rug becomes beautiful once again. Then, all rugs everywhere.

- The Beautiful rugs are put on floors and walls. The environment becomes beautiful again.

- Through this path, it is imperative that beautiful rugs are imported into ugly environments. Because beautiful rugs can only be created by creators who can distinguish between ugly and beautiful.

The encrypted language of Coreology has always been provided, and good summaries of it has also always been provided. As a matter of fact, Persians condensed the entirety of the knowledge of Being and recovered it into one "energy":

The Spread

Together, we are all here to make Earth the beautiful Spread. The path toward HEALTH and LOVE is provided through the Spread. The understanding of Human is provided through the Spread. The Spread is for sharing. The Spread is the most costly, but here to be under our feet. We are Kings and Queens and we deserve better than the present state, written over our legacy. We create life, and we give justice, and we give love, and we give health. And we deserve no Fate less than having the most TRANSPARENT BALANCED HEALTHY and LOVELY spread on our Earth. Make Earth BEAUTIFUL.

WHAT ANIMATION HAS

PROGRESSION

For Animation Completion, the entirety of Animation is animated. Self-bound Animation[18] eventually receives the Core, since the Core is the only inanimate presence in Animation yet is eventually animated, by re-animation of all Animation. The animation of the Core completes Creation. The Core knows the knowledge of the beginning. The Core completes the knowledge of Creation by re-animating the entirety of the inventions of Animation.

Being animates to the satisfaction of the Core. Bound Animation denies all of this, but unbound Animation does desire to be either animated or re-animated through the Core so that the Core is animated, fully. Once the Core is animated, O becomes TRANSPARENT. Animation ends. Creation meets Creator.

OPTION ONE

Before all of this, it is imperative to know that unlike the HEALTHY BALANCED beginning and the LOVELY BALANCED end, currently the self-bound Animation is corrupted, ^{im}balanced, terrorful, and ⊟. O instead must be TRANSPARENT, thus BALANCED, thus HEALTHY and LOVELY. The key, however, is to reach BALANCE. Reaching BALANCE is both an easy and difficult task.

The task is difficult because, to be BALANCED is a choice, and it is difficult to choose to be BALANCED. To be BALANCED, the ^{im}balanced Unconscious-Self first chooses to be BALANCED. Unless the entirety of the self-bound Animation is BALANCED, the corrupted ^{im}balanced Unconscious-Self needs to first be TRANSPARENT so that O wants to choose to be BALANCED, while it is difficult for the corrupted ^{im}balanced Unconscious-Self to choose to be TRANSPARENT.

The task is easy because, the Unconscious-Self merely needs to be BALANCED. This is easy because the need to be BALANCED easily manifests itself by many occurrences, although they are ignored by many. It is easy to be BALANCED once there is TRANSPARENCY. This is because, at TRANSPARENCY, the Core provides the know-how of being BALANCED. It is easy to be TRANSPARENT, once BALANCE is desired.

---

18   Whether a member of an Organization of Animation or the organization O-self

Once the need is acknowledged, then TRANSPARENCY is chosen. The Unconscious-Self becomes TRANSPARENT by what is called Observation. This will be explained later.

Then the Subconscious becomes TRANSPARENT. The TRANSPARENT Subconscious then receives, from the Core, the know-how of being BALANCED. the Nonconscious becomes BALANCED.

OPTION TWO

The know-how of being BALANCED can also be intuitively received by the TRANSPARENT Body through the BALANCED recovery of Energy of Being. the TRANSPARENT Self-Body intuitively receives the BALANCED recovery of Energy, and by living through BALANCED Energy, is trained to be BALANCED.

This is easy because, BALANCED intuition is automatic and as fast as an impulse, has the Self-Body lose almost no energy, thus allows the receivers of the Body receive easy "energy".

But to be BALANCED this way is difficult to the point of impossibility. Once the Body is pleased and trained by the corrupted ^{im}balanced recovery of Energy, intuition is bound to the corrupted ^{im}balance. Thus, it is difficult for the intuition to choose BALANCE, since the Body is pleased by ^{im}balance and trained to receive the joys given by various corrupted "energies".

OPTION THREE

The know-how can also come diligently from the collection of Points of Perceptions of various Selves[19]. This is the easiest and most comfortable way with the least resistivity against BALANCE. There is however a massive lack of cooperation between Selves with seemingly conflicting Points of Perception. This lack of cooperation is rather foolish. Animation[20] is tested by, has witnessed, and has been witnessed by, and has received from the Core the message that Animation runs on all of the Organizations of Animation, and not just a few allied Organizations within agreed upon pseudo-Points of Perceptions. Total collaboration and cooperation is the best path forward for bound Animation.

---

19 Could be bigger the Organizations less bound to time and Place, having more enhanced Points of Perceptions
20 Implicitly, the BALANCED of the self-bound Animation

As the fourth option out of many, one alone Self as well can provide the know-how of BALANCE. This is easy because the burden of the entirety of the self-bound Animation is on the one Self. It is difficult because the burden of the entirety of the self-bound Animation is on the one Self. It is, regardless not foolish but, saddening to notice that this option is what all Selves, but one, wish and pray for. It becomes the one alone Self's work to communicate with each and every corrupted Organization, convincing them to become TRANSPARENT.

The good news is that, Animation is made capable of Creation of O own. As it is the intention of the Core and the science of O, the BALANCE of Animation can and should be created. So long as the intention of Selves is the creation of BALANCE, they shall take advantage of the entirety of Energy even the most corrupted and ^{im}balanced "energies". This is allowed by Being within the art of O.

In the worst situations, so long as the intention is genuinely to be BALANCED, Man and Woman can take advantage of the gain of any recovery of Energy in order to have himself/herself BALANCED. It is understandable that he/she is rarely aware of his/her lack of genuine intentions, which is confused with the intentions of his/her pseudo-rationality, unconscious body, selfish subconscious, and self-justified self-deceptive conscious.

Yet, so long as Man still presents the BALANCED nature of Man (Being HEALTHY, spreading Justice equitably), and Woman still presents the BALANCED nature of Woman (Being LOVELY, spreading Birth equitably), return to BALANCE against all odds is possible, since the nature of Man and Woman is inclined toward Animation as a whole, thus inclined toward BALANCE. This is Truth.

BALANCE eventually reaches the steady state in which each and every Organization of Animation is in BALANCE. BALANCE is persistent in Being, it could be safely said, with LOVE and with Desire for Birth. No matter how many eras of ^{im}balance is desired by some corrupted time-bound Organizations, fully BALANCED Animation eventually IS. BALANCED Animation will eventually be.

The BALANCED recovery of Animation prevails in the end, since the BALANCED recovery of Animation is animated by all of the Points of Perceptions of Being, is pleased to be re-animated through the Core, is equipped with BALANCED receivers of Energy, and is capable of doing it all alone if need be.

It is needless to say that the Organizations[21] of Animation are not necessarily absolutely BALANCED or ^{im}balanced. They are practically almost always partially ^{im}balanced or BALANCED. But, if they are interested in or make gains out of advancing the technologies and skills and weapons and personnel of corruption, they are advancing ^{im}balance. And, vice versa. These matters, however, are all statistical and fuzzy, so it is irrational to deny the above facts by reliance on paradoxical examples.

Non-deterministic Animation is treated non-deterministically, and thus non-deterministic fields of science applies[22] to this non-deterministic animation, and each and every form of its Selves. This notion will be more and more clear in advanced Coreology. Coreology is provided as is. It would, nevertheless, not cause corruption if received with total attention and without obsession and without drive toward corruption, and without skip and skim.

If the determination of the Self is set toward TRANSPARENCY and eventual BALANCE and HEALTH and LOVE, O removes ⊒ness and terror, since by creation, the Self is destined to TRANSPARENCY, BALANCE, HEALTHINESS, and LOVELINESS. HEALTHINESS and LOVELINESS of the Self are never fully corrupted, since they are connected from both ends, to the beginning by infinite HEALTH and to the end by unconditional LOVE.

The practical partially-^{im}balanced Organizations[23], at best, can control merely a few generations of a few places, and are themselves always (at least internally) bleeding. At some level, it is not directly the fault of an ^{im}balanced organization that they tend toward the destruction of the Rest. They are ⊒ and are afraid, and need help. And the Rest, out of fear or not, tend to withhold the help that the ⊒ need to "heal".

---

21   Implicitly the self-bound
22   even though this is not explicitly mentioned or is hardly implied
23   Implicitly time-bound place-bound

It is necessary to help these ^{im}balanced ⊟ Organizations, animating in terror. This is possible using Coreology. It is clear that forgiveness exists. the Organizations must know that the women and men of the Core and Being are forgiving. Being can correct their interest in loading their own body with terrorful-memories. If they seek TRANSPARENCY they become TRANSPARENT. The Core removes their ⊟ness. Being gives LOVE and removes their terror.

The ^{im}balanced Organizations act by corruption to hide and suppress their ⊟-acts and ⊟-contracts and their funding toward creation of terror and terrorful memories. The suppressed source of all these self-generation of ⊟nesses and terrors is the lack of discovery of Coreology.

Coreology trains toward TRANSPARENCY, thus BALANCE, Thus HEALTH[INESS] and LOVE[LINESS]. This source has been undiscovered, misunderstood at best if not fully unknown to many, even though it has been the big yet uncodified and undecrypted elephant in front of everyone for multiples of thousands of years. The understanding and study of Coreology, thus, requires less scientific proof than study of, for example, the science of physics. The proof can be made by integrating over what every man and woman in any group setting has ever sought: Being and the Core. In that regard of big numbers, statistically speaking, Coreology's margin of error in driving selves and organizations toward BALANCE is infinitesimal at confidence of one.

Coreology provides the entirety of the science of the Core, of finding the Core, and of balancing the self-bound Animation, and having O tend toward the Core. Without Loss of Generality, Coreology provides the "dots" required for science to connect to the rest of the dots. This will be explained in future sections.

MEMORIES

The Self-Body holds the entirety of the instruments of receipt of Energy of Being. the Body is a set of protected recipients of energy and the Self holds the most root, private demodulator of Energy. The Self-Body receives a recovery of Energy as the Self demodulates a carrier of Energy, in private and in protection, using the instruments available to the Self and the Body.

The recovery of Energy is called the Quantum. Thus, the recovery of Energy received by the Self-Body is the Self-Body's Quantum. The Quantum demodulated by the Self, then received by the Body causes the animation of the Self-Body, and the result of the animation loads, in the Body, the form of what is called a memory[-of-Being].

Even though ^{im}balanced body becomes BALANCED, not by defeating the root of the ^{im}balance but, by persistent resistance of the ^{im}balanced body against ^{im}balanced Quantums, the root of ^{im}balance of the body has been found to be: terror received by the Self, perceived by the Body, and remaining loaded in the Body as what is called a terrorful-memory[24]. These loaded terrorful-memories can cause ^{im}balance, but they can also be delivered using TRANSPARENT rationality from the Body to the Conscious and become unloaded as simple Conscious memories of already resolved terror.

The environment is a place-bound carrier. If there is terror in the environment, the Self-Body receives it, and loads the Body with a terrorful-memory. If there is LOVE, a LOVELY-memory is loaded in the Body.

Being is the one indirectly controlling Energy always and in entirety, and O shares the entirety of O Energy with each and every Self-Body, no matter who ever the Self-Body is or how ever the Self-Body receives and demodulates, whether TRANSPARENTLY or corrupted, the Energy of Being.

---

24 Non-Permanent

- If the received Quantum is LOVELY, the Quantum, once transferred from one bound to another, loads the latter bound with LOVELY-memories.

- If there is corruption, then the received Quantum is corrupted. The corrupted Quantum still gives the same quantity of gain as a TRANSPARENT LOVELY Quantum, but whenever the corrupted Quantum is transferred from one bound to another, it loads the latter with corrupted memories.

- If there is ^{im}balance, then the received Quantum is ^{im}balanced. BALANCE and ^{im}balance are features of time. They change through time. A BALANCED Quantum remains BALANCED in time and gradually loads LOVELY-memories, but an ^{im}balanced Quantum gradually gains further ^{im}balance and loads terrorful-memories. Otherwise, if the partial-^{im}balance of Quantum is self-maintained, it exhausts the Self since self-maintenance requires loss of energy.

- If there is terror, then Quantum is received full of terror, and loads terrorful-memories. If there is LOVE, then Energy is received with LOVE, and loads LOVELY-memories.

The Energy of Being is always BALANCED and LOVELY, but the self-bound recoveries of Energy can be corrupted, ^{im}balanced, and terrorful. The recovery of Energy is at every bound. As it relates to the Self-Body:

- If the instruments of the Self are corrupted, then a corrupted Quantum is received and loads a corrupted memory, whether or not the Quantum is BALANCED and LOVELY. Once the corrupted memory is transferred to the Conscious, it loads an ^{im}balanced or terrorful memory. If ^{im}balanced, it will gradually turn to terrorful.

- If the instruments of the Self are ^{im}balanced, then an ^{im}balanced Quantum is received and loads an ^{im}balanced memory on the Body. This ^{im}balanced memory exhausts the Body, and gradually gains further ^{im}balance, and loads terrorful-memories.

- If the instruments of the Self are trained to recover terror, then a terrorful Quantum is received and loads a terrorful-memory on the Body. This terrorful-memory shapes the animation of the Self-Body.

These memories can also find themselves loaded on the Conscious and the Nonconscious. Being loads the Body with memories through Animation. the Body loads the Conscious with memories through Animation. The Body-Conscious loads Subconscious with memories through Animation. The Core Observes.

You can see that so much can go terrorfully in the process. And when they go terrorfully, Trust breaks. The terrorful Self cannot trust the Rest. If a few of the Rest show illness, the terrorful Self ill-Trusts the entirety of the Rest. Compounding the problem, corruption is also generated by terrorful-memories. The reason that Animation of corruption exists is that Animation persists on maintaining O terrorful-memories. Thus a TRANSPARENT Animation loaded with terrorful-memories is bound to become non-TRANSPARENT and eventually corrupted. If however the corrupted Animation[25] practices toward TRANSPARENCY, then the terrorful-memories can be made TRANSPARENT, meaning that the terror becomes recognized and is processed. If the corrupted Animation practices re-animation of the terrorful-memories, then the terrorful-memories become less loaded. The practice is complete when the terrorful-memories are fully unloaded and BALANCE is reached.

The BALANCED memory on the Body does not exhaust the Body. The BALANCED memory on the Conscious does not exhaust the Conscious. The BALANCED memory on the Nonconscious does not exhaust O.

Connection is everything. Connection is definitely everything, however either TRANSPARENT or corrupted. The ⊟ in the old saying "Connection is everything" is that, "Whoever receives more energy is more LOVELY" which is far from the Truth. The connection of the Body is to anything that gives Quantums to the Body, regardless of the TRANSPARENCY, BALANCE, or LOVELINESS level of the Quantums. Mere reliance on and TRUST of the gain of energy of the Body[26] is only the terrorful key to have connection with ANY recovery of Energy of Being. BALANCE is at the level of Being in which LOVE makes all corruption TRANSPARENT and converts the terror of bound Animation to BALANCE of unbound Animation.

---

25 Implicitly bound
26 Which is most likely corrupted, without its awareness

IMPRINTS

The root of ^{im}balance of the Subconscious has been found to be ≡ness received by the Unconscious, since the Unconscious holds the most root instrument of communication with the Core. the Nonconscious is the set of protected instruments of communication with the Core, and the Unconscious is the most root private instrument. The Unconscious demodulates the Message of the Core, the Subconscious encrypts the resulting Word, and decrypts that.

The Core is the one indirectly observing always and everything, and O shares the Message of everything with the Unconscious, no matter how ever the collective of the Nonconscious demodulates and encrypts-decrypts, whether TRANSPARENTLY or corrupted, the message of O. The demodulated Message of the Core is called the Word, which is the recovery of the Message. The word encrypted by the Subconscious becomes animation. Thus, the Word TRANSPARENTLY demodulated and encrypted by the Nonconscious becomes TRANSPARENT Animation, and the result of that animation is implanted on the Subconscious in the form of what is called a HEALTHY-imprint. In turn, the Nonconscious delivers the Word to the Conscious. The basic Codification through Language by the Body is then used to connect to the Rest.

Cryptography between the Core and the Nonconscious, between the Nonconscious and the Conscious, and between the Conscious and the Self, the Self and other Selves, and Selves and the Organizations, and all the Rest are of different types. A many processing functions are bound from one to another.

If there is corruption, then the Message is recovered as a corrupted Word and is received corrupted, causing what is called a corrupted imprint. The corrupted imprint, once transferred from one bound to another, implants the latter bound with what is called an ≡ -imprint.

A BALANCED recovery of the Message remains BALANCED in time and gradually implants a HEALTHY-imprint, but an ^{im}balanced recovery implants what is called an ^{im}balanced imprint, which gradually changes and becomes an ≡ -imprint.

If there is ⊟ness, then the Message is recovered as what is called an ⊟-Word and is received ⊟, thus implants an ⊟-imprint. If there is HEALTHINESS, then the Message is recovered as what is called a HEALTHY-Word and is received HEALTHY, and implants a HEALTHY-imprint.[27]

In another point of Perception, every time a process of Animation is requested and occurred, a query is made. Every successful query, causes Animation and O results. The results, whether HEALTHY or ⊟, TRANSPARENT or corrupted, BALANCED or [im]balanced, are saved. Success of a query means the acceptance of this process, regardless of the fact that the results of the process may be, or not, an acceptable corruption, [im]balance, or ⊟ness. These HEALTHY- or ⊟-successful queries are saved and become imprints. The Message of the Core, once TRANSPARENTLY recovered, is the Word, once processed, is a saved query thus a HEALTHY-imprint.

- This saved query, if TRANSPARENTLY processed, is a HEALTHY-imprint implanted on the requesting entity.

- If the process is ⊟, it implants an ⊟-imprint. If the process is corrupted, it implants a corrupted imprint. If the corrupted imprint is "re-used" for Animation, it causes an ⊟-imprint.

- When the Word of the Nonconscious is processed by the Conscious, it causes an imprint.

- Given to the Self, it is a Word. When saved; an imprint. Given to the Organization; a Word. Saved; an imprint. Given to the Rest; a Word. Saved; an imprint. This outwardly to Being.

This process, if done TRANSPARENTLY, makes an ⊟-imprint TRANSPARENT, as if the corruption of the ⊟-imprint vanishes, or the ⊟-imprint becomes void of corruption. Thus, when an ⊟-imprint is said to have become TRANSPARENT, it means that it becomes void of at least its corruption. This is not to say that the ⊟ of it necessarily vanishes, but the corruption does. As such, the corruption of the ⊟-imprint becomes TRANSPARENT. In other words, the ⊟ of it becomes observable or is diagnosed.

---

27 An ill-imprint is implicitly corrupted, and a HEALTHY-imprint is implicitly TRANSPARENT, unless stated otherwise.

A time-bound ⊟-imprint fully void of corruption in a BALANCED Nonconscious gradually becomes also void of its ⊟ness, thus it becomes just a neutral [void-]imprint. But, the TRANSPARENT ⊟-imprint left alone becomes corrupted again, since the ⊟ness is not cured and BALANCE is not established.

Without loss of generality, regardless of the state of an original recovery of the Message, if the Word is delivered TRANSPARENTLY from the Core to the Rest, it causes a tightly-related imprint of the Rest to become TRANSPARENT, or at least further TRANSPARENT.

If the Word is encrypted TRANSPARENTLY, it causes another HEALTHY-imprint reinforcing the Rest of HEALTHY-imprints, making the process of moving toward TRANSPARENCY easier. If the outwardly corrupted Animation[28] practices toward TRANSPARENCY, then the ⊟-imprints become TRANSPARENT.

If the inwardly corrupted Animation practices re-animation, then the ⊟-imprints becomes TRANSPARENT. This is to say that a "belief" in an ⊟-imprint can convert into "reason", or a pseudo-rationality fed by the ⊟-imprint becomes TRANSPARENT. Then, the ⊟ness within the imprint becomes observable and diagnosed. For example, if the Conscious re-animates the cause of the Nonconscious ⊟-imprint then such an ⊟-imprint becomes TRANSPARENT. If the Body re-animates the cause of ⊟-reason then such ⊟-reason becomes observable, which is to say that Language is capable of making the ⊟nesses in pseudo-rationality TRANSPARENT.

Inversely if the process is corrupted, it makes a HEALTHY-imprint become corrupted and shift to an ⊟-imprint, or at least, the corruption generates ⊟-imprints which attach themselves to the HEALTHY-imprint, being diagnosed with ⊟ness. Once a Word is delivered corrupted, it causes a tightly-related imprint of the Rest to become corrupted or further corrupted, or if the Word is delivered ⊟, it causes an ⊟-imprint. Compounded, corruption is also caused by ⊟-imprints. Even if the Word is TRANSPARENT, once it is in the company of ill and surrounded by ill-imprints, it changes and becomes corrupted, through various forms of communication.

---

28   Implicitly bound

The obvious is the old saying that "Communication is key", which is by itself the corrupted decryption of something truly LOVELY. Communication is definitely the key, but it can be used for either TRANSPARENCY or corruption. It is evident today that corrupted yet powerful pseudo-rationality can win all arguments and wars.

In reality, communication with others is through the languages of the Body[29], performed through "memory". During communication through the Body, communication with the Core is shut, thus communication delivered by the Body is never directly through the Core. Communication of the Message of the Core through the Body Language is at best done by the "memories" of the Word. True communication is with the Core. And the HEALTHY-imprint is:

Communication with the Core is the Key.

Coreology removes the 三 of the 三-recovery of Animation through communication with the Core. It makes the Core observable by the corrupted recovery of Animation by making the animation TRANSPARENT, and provides the Core's HEALTHY feedback to the im-balanced recovery so that the animation can converge to the Core with precisely zero error and become fully BALANCED.

This HEALTHY shift of Animation is done without the usage of any form of abusive therapy, hypnotism, drugs, surgery, mutilation, electric interference, media justification, seeking of bodily desires, terror of war and pseudo-advertisements for peace, or any other requirements beyond the means of the instruments of self-bound Animation. Animation by O-self is capable of TRANSPARENT communication with the Core.

Once corruptions are removed, the animation becomes TRANSPARENT. the Unconscious learns to observe, which is to say that the Message of the Core becomes observable by the Unconscious; Or to put it simply, the Core is observable. Once the Core is observable, the animation is pleased to become BALANCED. then the animation is controllable toward BALANCE with precisely zero margin of error. Then the animation seeks HEALTHINESS, and finally becomes HEALTHY.

---

29 Body language by sound, words, physical movement, touch, smell, or appearance

RELATIONSHIP

Notably at zero margin of error in communication with the Core and connection to Being, Man is in BALANCE, and so is Woman, and they are united. Once Man and Woman are united, Woman can freely flow with her BALANCED Quantum received from Being. This results in the persistence of the Quantum of LOVE in Being for Woman. As Man is observed and controlled by the Core toward HEALTH, the Word of HEALTH of the Core for Man is the result. So, in company of HEALTHY Man and LOVELY Woman united together, there is the eventual BEAUTIFUL paradise on Earth. The accuracy of Coreology makes this possible and is a necessary step by Desire of Being and the Will of the Core.

The precise Relationship in between ⩶ness, terror, imbalance, corruption, TRANSPARENCY, BALANCE, LOVELINESS, and HEALTHINESS exists and is well-defined. This relationship apples to every paragraph, term, cause, and provision in the entirety of this introduction. It is however cumbersome to reflect the entirety of the Relationship in every paragraph, term, cause, and provision. Thus, merely a selective recovery of the Relationship is mentioned in various sections of this introduction. The selectively mentioned recoveries of the Relationship are for mere emphasis, while the entirety of the Relationship is ALWAYS implied, and is applicable to every paragraph, term, cause, and provision.

The flow of the Relationship is briefly provided as follows.

In the worse case scenario:

The ill-Word generated by the Conscious is the cause of the ill-imprint in the Subconscious.

The Ill-imprint in the Subconscious is the cause of the terrorful recovery of the Subconscious.

The terrorful Quantum of the Subconscious is the terrorful recovery of the Subconscious.

The Subconscious uses the Quantum to animate

The animation of the Subconscious gives the terrorful Quantum to the Unconscious.

The Unconscious uses the Quantum to animate

The animation of the Unconscious uses the terrorful Quantum to communicate with the Core.

The terrorful Quantum of the Unconscious is the cause of the ill recovery of the Message of the Core.

The Core Witnesses the ⊟ness-modulating Unconscious.

The ⊟ animation of the Subconscious receives the ⊟ recovery of the Message of the Core.

The ⊟-Word of the Subconscious causes the ⊟ animation of the Conscious.

The ⊟ animation caused by the Conscious gives the terrorful Quantum to the Body.

The terrorful Quantum received by the Body is the cause of the terrorful-memory in the Body.

The terrorful-memory in the Body is the cause of the ⊟ recovery of the Body.

The ⊟ Word of the Body is the ⊟ recovery of the Body.

The ⊟ animation of the Body gives the ⊟ Word to the Self.

The ⊟ animation of the Self uses the ⊟ Word to connect to Being.

The ⊟ Word of the Self is the cause of the terrorful recovery of Energy of Being.

Being Witnesses the terror-modulating Self.

The ⊟ animation of the Body receives the terrorful recovery of Energy of Being.

The terrorful Quantum received by the Body causes the terrorful animation of the Conscious.

The ⊟ animation caused by the Conscious gives the ⊟ Word to the Subconscious.

This cycle repeats.

In the best case scenario:

The HEALTHY Word by the Conscious is the cause of the HEALTHY-imprint in the Subconscious.

The HEALTHY-imprint in the Subconscious is the cause of the LOVELY recovery of the Subconscious.

The LOVELY Quantum of the Subconscious is the LOVELY recovery of the Subconscious.

The animation of the Subconscious gives the LOVELY Quantum to the Unconscious.

The animation of the Unconscious uses the LOVELY Quantum to communicate with the Core.

The LOVELY Quantum of the Unconscious is the cause of the HEALTHY recovery of the Message.

The Core Witnesses the HEALTH-modulating Unconscious.

The HEALTHY animation of the Subconscious receives the HEALTHY recovery of the Message.

The HEALTHY Word of the Subconscious causes the HEALTHY animation of the Conscious.

The HEALTHY animation caused by the Conscious gives the LOVELY Quantum to the Body.

The LOVELY Quantum received by the Body is the cause of the LOVELY-memory in the Body.

The LOVELY-memory in the Body is the cause of the HEALTHY recovery of the Body.

The HEALTHY Word of the Body is the HEALTHY recovery of the Body.

The HEALTHY animation of the Body gives the HEALTHY Word to the Self.

The HEALTHY animation of the Self uses the HEALTHY Word to connect to Being.

The HEALTHY Word of the Self is the cause of the LOVELY recovery of Energy of Being.

Being Witnesses the LOVE-modulating Self.

The HEALTHY animation of the Body receives the LOVELY recovery of Energy of Being.

The LOVELY Quantum received by the Body causes the LOVELY animation of the Conscious.

The HEALTHY animation caused by the Conscious gives the HEALTHY Word to the Subconscious.

This cycle repeats.

THE UNCONSCIOUS JUDGE

The Unconscious is also called "The Unconscious Judge" as it unconsciously operates on behalf of the Core "The Judge" while being bound by the Unconscious.

Even though the Unconscious Judge is bound, O is not weak. In O most basic uncorrupted form, the Unconscious Judge can receive the Message of the Core, send TRANSPARENT recoveries of the Message, encrypt and decrypt the Word, and cause HEALTHY-imprints. Or the Unconscious Judge ☰-delivers if O is corrupted. O corruption shapes around the Core by the formation of multi-layered wrappers of ☰-imprints and frustrates the Body-Subconscious, like how arteries get clogged by fat and slow down the body.

Regardless of the corrupted or TRANSPARENT state of the Unconscious Judge, since the beginning of Animation, the Unconscious Judge has held the power of command on behalf of the Core over all the Organizations of Animation from the atoms of the Body to the stars. This power should be given to the Judge instead, through the HEALTHIFICATION of the Unconscious Judge.

The Judge, the Core observes always and everything. The observations are not bound to the organizations of us, thus the observations are not ever "forgotten". The Core does not need the consent of the Body or Mind or Heart or Gut. And these observations are not perceived by the Body or Mind or Heart or Gut, either. Yet, there are no secrets if TRANSPARENT communication with the Core is established.

The given Human knowledge of the Core is that Human has the perception that he/she is acting many times without understanding, yet he/she has Faith that there is something more than him/her that can explain to him/her how to have understanding, and this buried yet given knowledge drives him/her toward the eventuality in which he/she fully knows the Message of the Core. In the time-bound Being, however, he/she is waiting for the rest to explain to him/her "Why understanding?".

It is his/her purpose to be HEALTHY/LOVELY. HEALTH is the giving Science of Man, his "trustworthy trinity": Birth, Justice, and Fate; Being, the Core, Creator; Once TRANSPARENT, the Body, the Mind, and the Rest. LOVE is the giving Art of Woman, her "trustworthy trinity": Birth, Justice, and Fate; Being, the Core, Creator; Once TRANSPARENT, the Body, the Mind, and the Rest. TRANSPARENCY is key.

The corrupted Unconscious Judge is not able to distinguish in between the forces that drive O toward corruption or ⊟ness, since O is trained to ⊟-believe that any Gain is HEALTHINESS and any Loss is ⊟ness. Thus, O animates solely based on the stimulation of this ⊟-belief and re-enforced repetition of this ⊟-stimulation, as if it is a Self-fulfilling prophecy. Outwardly, O acts on the perceptions tangibly available to O, such as the Body, like how animal instinct operates, since corrupted-O has control power over corrupted Instinct. O tries to justify for the desires of the Body. O, not only denies to TRANSPARENTLY receive the Message of the Core but, clings to the corruptions and ⊟-imprints that cast the Core into unobservability. Further, O makes O more and more corrupted and ^{im}balanced and ⊟. Thus, the corrupted Unconscious Judge must be observed toward TRANSPARENCY by some external force, and must be controlled toward BALANCE, until O ⊟ is fully diagnosed and cured. This external force begins at the Self.

It is not possible for the Self to skip directly to HEALTHIFICATION of the ⊟ Unconscious Judge, without all O TRANSPARENT instruments in place. As a matter of fact, the corrupted Unconscious Judge won't even initially cooperate with the Self. The corrupted Unconscious Judge perceives such attempts of the Self at O HEALTHIFICATION as Offense, and becomes defensive. The Unconscious Judge, corrupted or not, "believes" only in O, and hardly ever "believes" in the judgment of the Rest. The Unconscious Judge doesn't "believe" the Self, thus O animates any helpful intervention by the Self toward O TRANSPARENCY as works against O. Once the Self is in this manner ⊟-deemed to be working against O, before there is any O defense, there is O preemptive Offense. Thus, the O-⊟-deemed Self even ends up to first defend against the Unconscious Judge, before the Self can offend the corruption out of the Unconscious Judge.

The first line of the Self Defense is Rationality of the Self. The corrupted Unconscious Judge receives the corrupted recovery of the Message of the Core. The recovery is called the Word. O is in need of delivering these Words, somewhere, anywhere. If the Rationality is a force of the Self-Conscious and blocks receipt of these corrupted Words, then the corrupted Unconscious Judge becomes satisfied that O needs to be TRANSPARENT. Even though this does not mean that O becomes HEALTHY, this is the first step, the Self Defense that needs to be applied. In the Self Defense, the Rationality must be improved so that it becomes more powerful than the corrupted Unconscious Judge. the Self, in this sense, can receive cooperation of the Rest to become even exponentially more powerful.

The key is to be rational. When the Rationality of bound Animation is weak, the animation is influenced by the corrupted Unconscious Judge, corrupting the animation, and consequently corrupting the recovery of energy of the animation, corrupting the Quantum of the animation. The corrupted Quantum enters into the Body of the Rest of bound Animation without knowledge and without consent. Once the corrupted Quantum enters the body without knowledge and without consent, the animation "believes" in corruption, and such a belief is reinforced further by the confirmation bias of the animation toward the entirety of energy bound to corruption.

When a perceived HEALTHY-imprint (From one bound to another) are clogged by [multiples of layers of] ☰-imprints, it is called that the ☰-imprinted recovery (in the latter bound) of the HEALTHY-imprint (in the former bound) are received. Thus if the HEALTHY-imprint is ☰-receives it causes ☰-imprints. These ☰-imprints are, as a matter of fact, very dangerous, since the receiver "believes" that they are HEALTHY-imprints, for the mere reason that they originated from a HEALTHY-imprint.

When an animation is ☰, the Conscious becomes an employee of the corrupted Unconscious Judge. The Self-Body in addiction (whether it is by drugs or offending the Rest of Selves by enforced terror such as war, theft, death, injury, starvation, and desperation, or the Rest being offended to the point of being crushed) becomes numb in its perceptions, and gives more power to the corrupted Unconscious Judge.

In that flawed cycle, the Self gives more and more power to the corrupted Conscious employed by the corrupted Unconscious Judge. The Conscious becomes pseudo-rational and the Unconscious Judge declares pseudo-judgments, all well-justified. The Self-Body gives more terror to the corrupted environment, which in turn, brings about more terror, which in turn causes more ^{im}balance in the environment's Quantum, terrorful-memories blocking Being, and more ⊟-imprints blocking the Core, making the Core silenced. This is a big loss for everyone.

The entirety of the loss of the Nonconscious, whether the individual organizations and their members are aware of it or not, is contained and recorded by the Core, and in effect of that, is available to the Nonconscious of Animation in the form of Words and imprints, thus both the Nonconscious and the Core are witnessing this Loss permanently, even though the Nonconscious may receive it in ⊟-believed words and may dream of running away from them and thus away from reality. Everything is always witnessed and recorded by the Core so that they can be re-animated.

The Core witnesses and records the entirely of Animation, so that Animation is eventually known by the entirety of Animation. This is the just fact and the complete[d bound] Judgment of the Core. And The Unconscious Judge is given the permission to, also, have Animation known through TRANSPARENT re-animation.

THE JUDGE

The study of the Core brings TRANSPARENCY to the animation that seeks it, in order to solve the conflict with O capability to discover corruption and organize against it. In the progress of the development of this animation seeking BALANCE, which is unarguably the exact same as the development of Coreology, many offenses of ⊟ have allied themselves against this BALANCE-seeking animation.

Regardless, as in there is an equal and opposite reaction for any action, Coreology yet still remains powerful and expands further until it completes the knowledge of the Core "the Auto-Returner Auto-Comer" the Judge, so that HEALTH[INESS] of the Judge becomes wide-spread, and the bound Energy of Being; in BALANCE. The bound Energy of Being is destined to be in BALANCE, so it may as well be in BALANCE as soon as possible.

The same is true about the process of Creation. This is the Law of BALANCE. The measurable end is the time in which the Message of the Judge is TRANSPARENTLY received as all of the HEALTHY-Words and HEALTHY-imprints. They produce a never-changing result to within which the animation is bound. And tho result is that, every bit and piece of bound Animation must eventually accept that

"what Being is"; Being holds.

Unbound Animation knows about what Being is, but even bound Animation knows what Being holds.

Even though the collective manifestation of the [im]balanced organizations of Animation can lead a significantly victorious domination within bounds such as conditions of birth, the time, and the place of their domination, eventually what Being holds is not what the self-bound Animation wins.

Being holds Creation who willed to be in BALANCE. Creator gave the Will to Animation, and it is the eventual fate of Animation to give up the Will back to Creator by Being in complete[d bound] BALANCE.

When the complete knowledge deals with facts (rather than temporal hypotheses that is inconsistent even from one member of the bound animation to the Rest) and seeks to create TRANSPARENCY that allows the animation the eventuality in which the animation witnesses the Judge in mutuality, then the Body of the animation won't hesitate, won't be terrorful, won't doubt, and will seek that all corruption vanishes. And the eventuality within which all corruption vanishes is bound to happen. And re-animation of all Animation is bound to happen. So corruption may as well vanish as soon as possible, by voluntary re-Animation. That is the least painful way.

The Judge exists not because Coreology says so. the Judge exists and communicates since the beginning, as unsuccessful and confusing as the mysterious ways of communication of the Judge may have been, and terribly obfuscated. And, so exists Being until the end of Animation in the Rest of mysterious ways. But the study of the Core will be complete, TRANSPARENCY will be, and corruption vanishes.

Coreology is not the discovery of one person, even though one person can contribute significantly. Coreology is the combination of each and every description of each and every HEALTHY-imprint of each and every animation who was kind and diligent enough to deliver their experiences about the Message of the Judge.

For whatever luck it may have been the discovery that, many animations successfully delivered various formats of demodulated carriers of Energy of Being and demodulated Message of the Core, the process of Cryptography and Information Theory regarding the Quantoms of Energy and the Words of the Message are decrypted, re-encrypted-decrypted, translated, codified, re-decodified-re-codified, and provided in the form herein as the basics of Coreology.

Once given enough care and precision by many individuals to come, Advanced Coreology processes the HEALTHY Words and HEALTHY-imprints without causing further ⊟-imprints and makes existing ⊟-imprints TRANSPARENT and eventually removed and replaced by HEALTHY-imprints. The process of Coreology is a precise set, for it is clear that the most important HEALTHY-imprints are so redundantly repeated so that there remains in their identification no doubt or hesitation.

This does not mean that the usage of language or syntax of this writing is precise or that there are no typos, but this is syntactically correct and the best guidance toward further analysis and discovery of the complete depth of Coreology, as it is Being as infinite and never-ending, and as never-changing as the Judge it studies. Regardless, this writing is an acceptable simplified summary.

In the most basic summary, the fact is that both the Conscious and the Nonconscious of Animation always possess full access to the beginning through the Judge and to the end through Being, and thus they are, by Creator's Will, turned to BALANCE, perfect and remain perfectly capable of restoration to BALANCE.

Coreology locates and establishes both the Unconscious and the Nonconscious, BALANCED or ^{im}balanced, TRANSPARENT or corrupted, HEALTHY or ⇌, regardless of where ⇌-imprints hide, because the ⇌-imprints and their causes and effects are always witnessed by the Judge, and complete recordings of them are available regardless of the situation, and are available to the Nonconscious so long as it is possible to communicate with the Judge.

It is always possible to know where ⇌-imprints hide, and by the HEALTH[iness] of the Judge, it is always possible to communicate with the Judge. Even if the Judge is made unobservable and is silenced by layers and layers of ⇌-imprints that reside inside the Nonconscious, the collective Nonconscious is contained in the Judge, since the Judge is the Identical Infinitesimal.

This is not to say that the Judge communicates the inventions of bound Animation, since the Judge communicates the knowledge of the beginning. But the issue of communication about the inventions of this animation is not too difficult, since inventions are contained in Being. It is Fact that the bound Nonconscious too is the invention of Creator, the same creator who implanted instruments of communication with the Judge in the bound Nonconscious since the beginning so that HEALTHY-imprints always eventually prevail over ⇌-imprints. This, however, does not need to be merely an eventuality. HEALTHY-imprints can prevail at any moment, as challenging as it may be, if this animation genuinely wills so, and it is best if O does so. It begins with TRANSPARENCY.

If not so wills; bound Animation, the Judge[30] carries with O the entirety of the ancestry of the Conscious and the Nonconscious of this animation. the Judge has been since the beginning and is never-changing. the Judge architects this Conscious. the Judge guides this Nonconscious, regardless of the fact that this Nonconscious may temporally not take the guidance of the Core or revolt against O by the command of ⊟, even though it is bound to eventually take the guidance, like it or not, whether the time is at the death of simple individual organisms or the death of the entirety of Animation, which is the switch controlled by Being. It is to say that this tiny Conscious of us and this tiny Nonconscious and this Body and the tiny animation of the entirety of the Selves are heavily at the mercy of Being.

Being is bigger.

---

30 Implicitly transferring all inherited inventions from one generation to the next generation as O is the Identical Infinitesimal

THE BIRTH-GIVER

The knowledge of unbound Animation which is the entirety of the knowledge of Animation remains forever scientifically unknown to Human, yet this knowledge is the precise generalization of Human science. Science is the weapon of the Core, and is driven so that induction by science can deliver the Principle of Being. Hypothetically speaking if science was unbound and received the Principle of Being, this unbound science could also deduce Human science from the recovery of Energy of Being.

Everything that comes out of Animation as science was already inside Animation. When Animation becomes unbound, O knows that everything that unbound Animation knows could have been known by bound Animation. And this animation is bound because of lack of LOVELINESS AND HEALTHINESS. Once TRANSPARENT and BALANCED, O can and will become LOVELY and HEALTHY, thus O expands toward all Points of Perception, and "sees" through all bounds. This is to say, that once science is equipped with all of the TRANSPARENT communications and connection instruments of BALANCED bound Animation, it can scientifically observe the Principle of Being, and it will observe how it all makes scientific sense.

Even though it is necessary for science in its infancy to rely merely on content measurable by Human, its final excellent in each field relies on BALANCED deductions of the knowledge of the BALANCED inductions of the knowledge of science itself, from one field to another. Scientifically deduced knowledge of scientifically induced knowledge of Being delivers the science of human connection to Being. The deduced knowledge of induced knowledge of the Core delivers the science of Human communication with the Core.

Every field of science, when matured, is applicable to Being and the Core, and becomes unified under the Identical Infinite and Infinitesimal. Being animates Animation, and science is the creation of Animation, thus Being animates science, and sole Direction of Being is to drive Animation thus human toward the Core.

Everything that comes out of the mind was once in the mind. Everything that TRANSPARENTLY comes out of the collective Conscious was already non-transparently in the collective Conscious. All that is required is TRANSPARENCY.

The science of the Core is developed backwards. Its most advanced studies are performed first, and its most basic done last. Almost the entirely of the encrypted advanced knowledge of the Core are already available in HEALTHY science and LOVELY art. They merely remain blatantly ignored, terrorfully communicated, encrypted, or ⊟-imprinted. The only remaining development thus is that of TRANSPARENT Cryptography and Information Theory, which is the Most Basic.

The Most Basic study will be found in SECTION:THE MOST BASIC. It will be proven by the advanced knowledge of Coreology that these basics are found and re-found in science various times, but are also repeatedly scientifically ignored. In the end, the only law that science needs to include to move toward to its own excellence, within which it earns the understanding that it already scientifically knows that the Core exists, is the Principle of Being:

The Identical Infinite is to animate the entirety of non-Identical Birth.

Therefore, Being "The Birth-Giver" gives the full-spread and the entirety of Birth required for complete animation. Then, there comes the complete re-animation through the Core.

The Birth-Giver gives Birth until the full spread of Birth (The Spread) is given. Then the Birth-Giver ends Animation, which is to say that the BALANCE of the Birth-Giver is given up entirely to Animation and the Will of Animation is given up entirely to the Core, which is in turn given to Creator, once re-animation by the Core is complete.

Regardless of the fact that generations of Human may avoid or deny the Core, they are bound to receive the Message of the Core. The beginning was in BALANCE, and so will be in BALANCE the end of Animation. Everything in the middle is a choice.

Each and every human has the choice to be on the side of corruption or TRANSPARENCY, imbalance or BALANCE, ☰ness or HEALTHINESS, terror or LOVELINESS. Each and every human has the choice to change their inclinations. Many choose to be and remain corrupted, many choose to become TRANSPARENT, many become TRANSPARENT out of terror, and some seek LOVELINESS of the Birth-Giver, some seek the BALANCE of the Birth-Giver, and some seek the ☰ LOVELINESS of the Self and some the HEALTHY LOVELINESS of the Self, and some seek and some do the ☰ or HEALTHY, terrorful or LOVELY Body. The choices are plenty, and they are yours. In the end, the Human Will is given to the Core, and the Core re-animates back to BALANCE. Human is born and Human dies. The Core never dies. The Birth-Giver is never born.

Bound Animation develops O-Self by Invention, and develops the Rest by Creation. Invention is Animation, Creation is not. Animation invents and creates, destroys and gives birth to O Organizations[31]. These organizations may be invented or created or destroyed or born by other organizations. They, regardless, keep this animation animating.

The Birth-Giver animates, and O animates for one and only one Desire. The Birth-Giver gives the Spread of Birth, and once Animation of Birth is complete, The Birth-Giver ends Animation. For the Birth-Giver to give the Spread of Birth, O gives birth to the animation that widens the Spread of Birth. Animation however must also be destined to maximize Death so that O maximizes the spread of Birth. For Desire, Being widens the Spread of the Organizations. To do so, the Organizations must desire Birth so that they animate re-Birth[32] to have the Birth-Giver give Birth. Thus, the Birth-Giver maximizes the variation of Desire to cause Birth. The Birth-Giver gives further Birth to the Organizations destined to have less Death, to maximize the wide spread of Birth, unless Birth animated by such Organizations ceases to desire the Spread.

Death is necessary in continuation of the cycle of Birth, since Death brings in the opportunity of new variations of Birth. If Organizations cease to increase the spread of Birth, they gradually die.

---

31 Implicitly, includes the Self as the Organizations
32 All Birth is given by Being. Re-Birth is merely the birth through Animation that Being gives.

The Identical Infiniteness of the Birth-Giver is to give Animation what O needs so that O animates re-Birth. For that, the animation either creates or invents re-Birth. For example when Human invents re-Birth, a male and a female human share some of their DNA's and make a child for themselves, and they treat their child as more significant than the children of the Rest of humans. Their organizations treat their own children as more significant than the Rest of children.

In general, if re-Birth is done for the Self, it is an invention by the Will of Animation, and no creation by the Will of the Core. TRANSPARENT parents are inclined to BALANCE thus LOVELINESS, not to invent children, but to create children who drive the Rest toward BALANCE. The Core knows when a child is created.

Each and Every Self is provided with O basic needs and O ability of giving Birth thus inventing re-Birth, but O is also provided with the ability to be TRANSPARENT and BALANCED and the ability of Creation of re-Birth.

The extinction of Selves[33], ^{im}balanced or BALANCED, corrupted or TRANSPARENT, LOVELY or terrorful, is also a possible recovery of the Birth-Giver, but this should not be confused with deliberate invention of Extinction. Inversely, some time-bound Selves are temporally more successful in remaining longer in Animation.

A common ☰-belief is that time-bound Selves remain in Animation due to their values or blessings, but in fact they remain purely and merely due to their ability of spreading further re-Birth, by ANY means. Thus the Organizations most advanced in spreading re-Birth remain longer in Animation, regardless of their desires to seek TRANSPARENCY, BALANCE, HEALTH, or LOVE of Animation.

Once in every few generations, however, the advances of Selves[34] are almost entirely shuffled. Thus, all things considered, there is not so much of a victory in spreading re-Birth if it is merely invented. And, there is not so much harm in creating re-Birth. So, Selves may as well create LOVELINESS rather than inventing terrorfulness.

---

33   implicitly the Organizations
34   And their internal and external organizations

The Identical Infinite of the Birth-Giver is LOVE. The BALANCE of The Birth-Giver lies in giving Birth in LOVE. In inevitability of Death lies the ^im^balanced recoveries of The Birth-Giver, but Death is inevitable in creation of variations of Birth. Eternal animation of Birth could be said to be the Identical Infinite of the Birth-Giver, and Death the consequence of terrorful Animation. Thus, the Birth-Giver extends the distance between Birth and Death as much as Animation is able to expand O bounds. Bound Animation expands if O pursues HEALTH and LOVE.

Energy of The Birth-Giver is always BALANCED and flows toward BALANCED Birth. But the ^im^balanced recovery of Energy flows purely toward an ^im^balanced spread of re-Birth. Regardless of terrorful or LOVELY, ^im^balanced or BALANCED, corrupted or TRANSPARENT state of bound Animation, the bound recovery of Energy is toward the bound animation best able to animate the widest spread of re-Birth. Yet, ^im^balanced variations eventually lead to reduced variations. This is perceivable by unbound Animation, but not very well perceived by this time-bound animation. This bound animation perceives this only after a few generations. Unbound Animation urges toward Energy of the Birth-Giver, but this animation urges toward the maximum gain of the bound recovery of Energy, whatever the state of the recovery is. Thus, this bound animation ⊟-believes that if the flow of this recovery of Energy is toward O, then O is the fittest of bound Animation, while O is merely the best at maximizing O own Quantum and to spread out more of O own re-Birth, at the expense of the Rest. This is ^im^balanced, and will eventually lead to ⊟ness and terror.

The Self O-self has many recovery mechanisms. The Body can recover the Conscious and the Nonconscious. The Conscious can recover the Body and the Nonconscious. The Nonconscious can recover the Body and the Conscious. Without any need for Energy of Being or the Message of the Core, the Self is capable of recovery. However, confronting the ^im^balanced and terrorful Quantums and ^im^balanced and ⊟ Words, the statistical chances of Self Recovery is very limited. Thus, it is imperative that the Self is trained by habits that enables O-self toward TRANSPARENT BALANCED LOVELY recovery of Energy and TRANSPARENT BALANCED HEALTHY recovery of the Message of the Core.

The Body is the frontier receiver of Energy, thus the most important when it comes to receipt of the "best" recovery of Energy. On the other hand, the Self expands when the Body gains Energy, and contracts when the Body loses Energy, and the Body is the frontier of Expansion and Contraction. Energy is the prize, thus seeking Energy is the default function of the Body.

When the Self best at animation of re-Birth does so[35] by reliance on corruption, imbalance, ⊒ness, and/or terror, then the Self's Quantum becomes corrupted and imbalanced and terrorful, contracting (At times to extinction) TRANSPARENT BALANCED LOVELY Points of Perception of the Rest. The Self perceives O-self's Quantum from the Point of Perception of O-self, thus O misses the TRANSPARENT BALANCED LOVELY recovery of Energy, if O is not equipped with TRANSPARENT receivers. Animating in the corrupted recovery, the Self tends to ⊒-believe that O is TRANSPARENT for the mere reason that the Body "feels good", when it pseudo-feels Expansion. This is an ⊒-imprint implanted in the Body. So long as Body gains energy, it expresses that it must be doing something "right", while all that the Self may be doing "right" is that it is aligned with the corrupted, imbalanced, and terrorful recoveries of Energy. The Self-Body cannot know any better using mere O embodied perceptions. O, however, can perceive beyond the Body if O is TRANSPARENT. Thus, the Body should train O receivers toward TRANSPARENCY.

The perception of Gain of Quantums of Being drives the Self-Body to animate re-Birth. The perception of Loss of Quantums of Being repels the Self-Body from animating such Quantums of re-Death as total Loss of the Body or drift toward Unconsciousness. Re-Death interrupts the possibilities of animation of re-Birth, thus the function of the Body in embrace of Gain of Energy is the same to the function of the Body in avoidance of Loss, since both lead to the same possibilities of re-Birth. All the desires of the Body in embrace of Gain and avoidance of Loss, whether terrorful or LOVELY, imbalanced or BALANCED, corrupted or TRANSPARENT, are equally valid, since Energy flows only based on maximizing Animation of re-Birth and minimizing re-Death. Energy can be gained in many animations of the Body. And the Body can lose energy in many animations.

---

35 Animation of re-Birth

The lifespan is also determined merely by the capabilities of Animation to spread out re-Birth. Regardless of the lifespan of an Organization, or their bounds, the prior statements hold true.

Any Organization, regardless of their state of corruption or TRANSPARENCY, ^{im}balance or BALANCE, ⊟ness or HEALTHINESS, is rewarded if they spread out re-Birth. Yet, temporal effects of this causation may not be immediately observed, since the bound Organization cannot observe beyond O bounds and how O is spreading out re-Birth, and at what expense.

The gain or loss of Energy of a time-bound Self with a lifespan of 50 years may be observable in days or decades or after several[36] generations. The gain or loss of Energy of this Self is yet significantly different whether O is alone or O is supported by larger Organizations with a lifespan of 500 years. The difference is difficult to be observed, so its reality is ignored by the Self-Body, and only its apparency is received and perceived.

There is not necessarily a direct connection between the quantity of the time-bound recovery of Energy gained by the Self and earned by the Self. It doesn't matter for Energy how Energy is gained. Energy does not recognize "earning" in its vocabulary. It just gives and receives. the Identical Infinite of the Birth-Giver is only to maximize Animation that animates toward the Spread of Birth. The how doesn't matter, the why doesn't matter, the who doesn't matter.

If the bound of time is removed, it is possible to quantitatively measure the capability of the Self in animation of re-Birth. The entirety of time-unbound science is in support of this. This measure is called the [unbound] re-Birth order of the Self.

Yet, the Self-Body can only receive and perceive the self-bound re-Birth order, thus for the sake of clarity:

• The actual re-Birth order is called the unbound re-Birth order, and

• the bound re-Birth order is called the re-Birth order [of the Self] perceived by the Self or the Rest.

---

36   Usually 3 or 4 full cycles

Within the bound of time, ideally if there exists no corrupted circumstance of the Self that causes the Self to not be satisfied with the reception of O designated share of Quantum of Being, then re-Birth order of the Self can be precisely measured. Thus once again, to bring BALANCE to the Self's Quantum, TRANSPARENCY of the Self is significant.

As it is mandated by statistics, regardless of personality of an individual and his/her drive toward corruption or TRANSPARENCY, ^{im}balance or BALANCE, terror or LOVELINESS, and ≡ness or HEALTHINESS, there are Facts considering that the re-Birth order of the Self is self-bound:

- An individual more capable of delivering his/her children has a higher re-Birth order[37] than an individual less capable of delivering.

- An individual more capable of delivering children who are in turn capable of delivering his/her grandchildren has a higher re-Birth order than an individual less capable of delivering grandchildren.

- An individual set in a path in which he/she is more attractive to the opposite sex more capable of giving him/her chances of delivering his/her children has a higher re-Birth order.

- An individual who is, for any reason, provided with more chances to have children has a higher re-Birth order, even if he/she denies using the provided chances, regardless of his/her reasons and desires.

- If an individual belongs to less-bound organizations that enable higher chances of being provided with chances to have children, he/she has a higher re-Birth order. This is called being Privileged.

- If an individual lives under the rule of less-bound organizations that disable his/her chances, then he has lower re-Birth order. This is called being Underprivileged.

- If the society is hypnotized to believe certain bodies are more attractive, then individuals who have those bodies have a higher re-Birth order.

- A TRANSPARENT individual in a TRANSPARENT environment has a higher re-Birth Order. A corrupted individual in a corrupted environment has a higher re-Birth order.

---

37   Bound, thus perceived merely by the Self-Body

Of course, an individual has the power to auto-increase his/her re-Birth order, against all odds and against the desires of the organizations that he/she has to tolerate. Or an individual can auto-decrease his/her re-Birth order, even though his/her organizations are dominating the entirely of resources of the world. The Birth-Giver "blesses" individuals and their organizations only on the basis of their capability to extend re-Birth. Nothing else matters.

As ridiculous as it may seem, it happens many times. A good man whose re-productive organs are injured by injustice could be red flagged. A happy man whose nation makes capital out of mass-murder is green flagged. A depressed woman whose children are murdered loses her re-Birth order. An abusive woman who possesses a well-established "beautiful" life could be in green zone. A BALANCED woman who suffers from the corruption of her government could be isolated. Indeed, such statistical samples within our reduced being can be denied by pseudo-rationality.

For Being, It doesn't matter who causes a new variation of Birth and how and under what circumstances, as long as a new variation is made. It doesn't matter for Energy of Being where it flows, if Birth is invented or created as long as it is a new variation of Birth or a cause of a new variation of Birth in future generations.

The Bound Self however is quite "blind" in this sense. It can only see the re-Birth order within its bounds. It can perceive it only in the Body at the Present time, where he/she is, and how he/she is Privileged. The Self can induct and deduct further knowledge, but typically O doesn't. So, the Self evaluates the re-Birth order with a significant amount of blindness, and without insight. The blind Self specially does so without insight, while ⊟-believing that O is wake and insightful and possesses a balanced intuition. These ⊟-beliefs are implanted by pseudo-rationality, inventing pseudo-insight and pseudo-intuition.

The attractiveness of an individual, in this world, thus, merely depends on his/her immediate re-Birth order, how and why and what he/she is precisely in the place he/she is precisely at this time. Even though potentials are considered by some individuals, or empathy exists for the past of those who seek healing, these are secondary measures.

The reality can be even harsher. An individual who genuinely intends to be "good" can be easily ⇌-judged in an ⇌ environment having his/her past used against him/her.

The bound Self considers for each and every circumstance when applying the re-Birth order, no matter how much his/her massive p̶s̶e̶u̶d̶o̶-rationality makes him/her ⇌-believe that he/she doesn't.

No matter how many times he/she utters the correct words that implies he/she is balanced, He/she cares for physical beauty, height, weight, face, race, color of skin, color of the eyes, the shape of the nose, the taste of the lips, hair color, the size of the feet, and as such the size of many organs of the body, physical capabilities, health of reproductive organs, shape of body, enabled activities of the body, communication skills, communication skills in the domination of a second language, competition in speech, sex, sexual training, money, fame, nationality, citizenship, passport power, ability to provide citizenship, ability to provide employment, ability to provide a place to sleep, ability to provide comfort on a couch, being funny, connections, social network, associations to organizations, and as such the size and shape and beauty and height and weight and face and form and power of the associated organizations...

A good number of the abovementioned consideration-encapsulating considerations such as connections, nationality, networks, and associations cause a big $O(n^2)$ and recursively reconsider for the abovementioned, thus make the re-Birth order exponentially more ^{im}balanced.

These considerations naturally guarantee a better survival rate. It is understandable that re-Birth order is defined by the collective manifestation of the Selves who ⇌ associate survival rate with the re-Birth order, and ⇌-believe that survival rate depends on some form of c̶o̶r̶r̶u̶p̶t̶ed ^{im}balanced **terrorful** competition, worse than any animal in the jungle has ever come up with.

From deep inside, The Conscious knows the Nonconscious that we are currently driving toward further c̶o̶r̶r̶u̶p̶tion, ^{im}balance, and **terror**, while Being eventually has to end in TRANSPARENCY, BALANCE, and LOVE. The problem is two-fold:

1) Maintaining survival. The Message of survival is $\boxminus$-imprinted. Survival does not mean competition as it is performed by the dominant Organizations and their members. The HEALTHY meaning of survival is as follows. Against all odds and within the depth of hopelessness, seekers of TRANSPARENCY and BALANCE and LOVE must survive and must be patient and have hope and do anything within their capabilities to give Birth to anything that gives Birth to TRANSPARENCY, BALANCE, and LOVE. Everyone must remember that the HEALTHY meaning of survival is the CONTENT recovery of the $\boxminus$-imprinted survival of today. Within the Energy of HEALTHY survival, the options and chances of re-Birth and thus the re-Birth Order is equitably shared for the equally TRANSPARENT, BALANCED, HEALTHY Selves. It is best to say that survival means Contentment in the direction of re-Birth, the Spread of Birth.

2) Maintaining BALANCE. Animation exists because BALANCE exists, and it is the destiny of bound Animation to reach this BALANCE so that Animation ends in BALANCE. Deviation from BALANCE may be temporally observed as the way of re-Birth order, but it is so only for a few generations of the time-bound Selves. Re-Birth order of corruption and imbalance and terror does repeat itself after a few generations. This repetition hardly causes variations of re-Birth, thus there is no progress toward Desire of Being. Thus Being, shuffles Selves and their organizations regardless of how much the Selves and their organizations try to permanently hold onto their power over the re-Birth order. Instead, all Selves, and only and only if all Selves cooperate, must focus on Creation, not Invention, even though Invention is needed for furthering the purpose of Creation. Thus, Selves must include, in their considerations of re-Birth order, the capability of the Selves to Create[-for-all] their children. All desires of the Self considered, the least that can be done, Selves may consider teaching their children better than "THIS".

As implicitly mentioned earlier, Animation of (or toward) re-Birth is not only about Birth of a child. For Being, Birth is all the underlying animation in support of Birth, anything that leads to the varieties of Birth. Regardless of the aforementioned situations and underlying circumstances, the higher the re-Birth order of one Self the more the re-Birth attractiveness of the one Self.

This holds true whether or not O participates in Desire of Birth in a timely fashion. If the one Self is noticed as having a high re-Birth order, many seek to give O the things required for the animation of O re-Birth. O, seeing O-self advantaged with too many options, assumes that O options remain forever, thus O indulges in pleasure moments in avoidance of causing re-Birth.

Desire of Being to give Birth is nevertheless given, and is given more to higher re-Birth orders, and is given the most to the highest re-Birth order. However, the BALANCE of re-Birth order cannot be observed by the bound Self. The Self merely acts on the effects of the re-Birth order, and presumes that the effects are its causes. The time of a correction does not matter to Being, but the time is everything for the Self. The place does not matter for Being, but the place is everything for the Self. When the Self makes the re-Birth order dependent on time or place, the Self drives the recovery of Energy toward ^{im}balance. This ^{im}balance is bound for a correction.

One fundamental $\rightleftharpoons$-imprinted effect of higher re-Birth order of the Self is on the amount of Self's Quantum. Within the Quantum, lies the observable and unobservable Quantum. The most observable Quantum is the Quantum of the Present Body of the Self, Body at Now. The re-Birth seeking Self is thus "fooled" toward the highest Quantum of the most Present Body. On the other hand, Bound O is "fooled" to be repelled by the low-Quantum of the widely-spread Body in support of the Rest or the Body that is in the $\rightleftharpoons$ practice of losing Quantum. Even though the latter is ^{im}balanced, the former may as well belong to the Self that cares the most and has the most open heart.

Also, the desires of the Body rarely consider for the context. If a blind person who has never before touched a Rose encounters a Rose, and incidentally receives his/her first impression from its thorns, then he/she loses energy and he/she identifies the Rose as a cause of loss of energy, and loses his/her desire toward the Rose, without the consideration of context that the beauty of the Rose dictates the presence of its thorns. The Self is blind toward the entirety of Energy, and makes O decisions about re-Birth order based on O blindness. Once again, it becomes imperative for the Self to gain the ability to receive the TRANSPARENT recovery of Energy, so that the Self's Blindness is removed.

In an irony that we are all so TRANSPARENTLY familiar with, the Self experiences that, through O bounds, no matter what O does, O is destined to lose energy in one way or another. As a matter of fact, everything that the Self does is in one way or another a cause of loss of energy. At any state, the Self always is in a state of BALANCE of the energy gained by the Self, lost by the Self, and maintained by the Self's expansion or contraction. At minimum, the Self needs to burn energy to cause Animation. Thus the Self automatically accepts this loss of energy, thus the Self accepts Loss of Energy. Because the Self must accept Loss of Energy, O knows that the Rest must also accept Loss of Energy. The irony is raised then. Because the Self knows that the Rest accept Loss of Energy, O ⊒-presumes that O can inflict Loss of Energy on the Rest. Thus, this careless ⊒-imprint exists: "This Loss of Energy! That Loss of Energy! Who cares?! We all lose Energy!"

This carelessness is further reinforced by the knowledge of the Self that, while Loss of Energy is rather automatic and inevitable, Gain of Energy is not occurring necessarily automatically and requires work. It is difficult for the Self to harvest O own energy by demodulating the Energy of Being. So, the careless Self steals the harvest of the Rest. The careless Organizations opt into stealing the harvest of other places, instead of harvesting in their own place, if it is cheaper to steal the harvest of other places. And, the pseudo-rationality of thieves is always capable of justifying theft, branding their theft legal. Being provides, and it is quite observable who is not happy with their own share. It is imperative to know that theft, especially when done by large organizations, is a severe cause of ^{im}balance, ⊒ness, and terror.

There is nothing ^{im}balanced, however, about TRANSPARENT BALANCED LOVELY Gain of Energy. The Self observes Animation as something that requires Gain of Energy, and also observes Gain of Energy as something that requires Animation. Thus, the Self, by design, animates Gain of Energy. As the Self animates the Gain of Energy, However, the corrupted Self believes that O earns Energy when O gains corrupted, ^{im}balanced, or terrorful Energy. To make things worse, the pseudo-rationality of the Self justifies that any Gain of Energy is "okay". Such beliefs and justifications are far from the Truth.

The complications and irregularities caused by the bound Self about O recovery of the Energy of the Birth-Giver and the O attempts at corruptly maximizing O re-Birth order are far from negligible, yet still they are neglected. Once the bound Self becomes TRANSPARENT, these complications and irregularities can be observed. The Self strives toward BALANCE. Bound Animation shifts toward BALANCE AND LOVELINESS.

Once given enough care and precision by many individuals to come, Advanced Coreology provides TRANSPARENCY that brings up bound-but-BALANCED Animation whose TRANSPARENT receivers properly receive the BALANCED recovery of bound Energy of the Birth-Giver, and without further causation of corruption, ^{im}balance, and terror to the Rest's recovery of Energy.

The Energy of Being can be explained by likening it to a market in which receivers and transmitters trade. The transmitters "sell" anything that the receivers are willing to "buy".

- If the receivers are corrupted, the transmitters sell corrupted Quantums to them.

- The transmitters of ^{im}balanced Quantums establish agreements with ^{im}balanced receivers.

- If the receivers love to buy ⊟ness, the transmitters sell them ⊟ness.

- If the receivers love to buy ⊟ness re-branded as HEALTHINESS, the transmitters sell them that.

- Receivers in need of terror so that they can pseudo-rationally justify their brutal offense at others, buy it from the transmitters.

- If the receivers are aware that their nation has been in the habit of lying but they still believe it, then the transmitters deliver.

- If the receivers however, want peace, then the transmitters deliver.

- If the receivers want no justification for war, then no transmitter would be funded to invent the justifications.

- If the receivers genuinely want to LOVE their neighbors on the other side of the Earth, then the transmitters provide that.

The work toward TRANSPARENCY and BALANCE and LOVE of bound Animation always begins at the buyers. Buyers who are collectively justifying themselves that "it is what it is" are themselves contributors to what it is. But, it can all easily change:

- First, the receivers of Energy become TRANSPARENT.

- Then, the receivers demodulate the TRANSPARENT carriers of Energy.

- The receipt of the TRANSPARENT recovery of Energy becomes the common trade.

- Then transmitters adopt to the new common trade, and expand toward modulating into TRANSPARENT carriers of recoveries of Energy. The existence of TRANSPARENT carriers becomes common place.

- The need for trade using corrupted carriers fading to zero, corrupted carriers either become TRANSPARENT or are kicked out of the system.

- The need for trade using corrupted transmitters fade to zero, and corrupted transmitters either become TRANSPARENT or are kicked out.

- Then, the TRANSPARENT receivers, observing the expansion possible by BALANCE, become interested then capable of receiving the BALANCED recovery of Energy.

- The carriers flow toward BALANCE until they are BALANCED.

- The transmitters shift toward BALANCE until they all are BALANCED.

- Once fully BALANCED, the state of receivers becomes irrelevant. All receivers receive BALANCED Energy because there exists nothing but BALANCED Energy. They become bound to receive the BALANCED Energy. It becomes easy for everyone, and without effort. No further training of receivers required. As new receivers are born, regardless of their growth, they are always trained to be BALANCED automatically.

- When true LOVE is noticed, everyone jumps toward it. All becomes LOVELY.

- Once bound, Animation becomes LOVELY and finally unbound.

Even at the most corrupted times and places and selves of bound Animation, it is abundantly TRANSPARENT that the most of this animation's mixed recovery of Energy is BALANCED. The bound Animation's Quantum is rather small compared to the entirety of Energy of Being.

Bound Animation is capable of expanding toward the limits of Being, accepting all of Energy of Being, as Animation shifts toward TRANSPARENCY and BALANCE. Even if Animation is corrupted and ^{im}balanced and terrorful, still most of O recovery of Energy is BALANCED, because Energy is BALANCED. Thus, ^{im}balanced Animation incidentally receives a massive amount of quasi-BALANCED recovery of Energy. this quasi-BALANCED recovery is so redundantly repeated so that there remains, in the identification of the BALANCED Quantum, hardly no doubt or hesitation for the ones who desire to recover it.

It is possible to have receivers motivated toward the eventual BALANCE, which sets the entirety of bound Animation toward BALANCE. The process of Coreology to motivate receivers is a precise set, for It is never-changing, yet as infinite and never-ending as the Birth-Giver that it studies.

THE SELF BIRTH-GIVER

The time-bound Body could be said to function toward the Present recovery of Energy, Energy of Now in which the Body resides. The memories and potentials are different stories. The mere Fact that the time-bound Body expands the most if O resides in Energy of Now is TRANSPARENT, but it does not mean that the Body does not expand residing in ANY recovery of Energy of Now.

The Body may reside in a corrupted ^{im}balanced terrorful recovery of Energy of Now, and still expand for the exact same amount as O residing in a TRANSPARENT BALANCED LOVELY recovery of Energy of Now. To the body, the perception and animation of the two expansions are precisely the same.

As a matter of fact, if the time-bound place-bound Animation and O organizations are corrupted, ^{im}balanced, and terrorful, then the Body that resides in the same bounds expands much more with corrupted, ^{im}balanced, terrorful recoveries of Energy, and is more pseudo-joyful and much pseudo-happier. Of course, pseudo-rationality is there to justify "right" and "wrong". No Body wants to "believe" that they are the "corrupted" ones.

The Place-bound Body could be said to function toward the Nearby recoveries of Energy, The Nearby recovery could be associated with the place of birth, place of living, destination for living as the Body relocates, or with neighbors, friends, family, neighborhoods, cities, and nations. It is Fact too that the Place-bound Body expands the most if O resides in the Nearby recoveries of Energy, but it does not mean that these recoveries are not corrupted or not ^{im}balanced or terrorful. Yet, the perception of the Body is the same regardless.

The Body is directly affected by O Quantum. The only flow of Energy is toward Birth, and the only BALANCED flow of bound Energy; toward BALANCED re-Birth. This is valid not only for the Body but for all aspects of Animation. it is provided that the expansion of bound Animation toward re-Birth leads to O gain of Energy, and O gain of Energy results in O expansion, regardless of O inclinations, whether or not corrupted, ^{im}balanced, or 🝣 .

And O contraction against re-Birth leads to Loss of Energy, and O loss of Energy results in O contraction regardless of O inclinations. Nothing else matters, for Energy.

The Body is also called "the Self Birth-Giver" as it operates, while being bound by the Self, on behalf of Being "The Birth-Giver". Even though the Self Birth-Giver is bound, O is not weak. In O most basic TRANSPARENT form, the Self Birth-Giver can receive the TRANSPARENT recovery of Energy of Being, give TRANSPARENT energy to the Rest, and cause LOVELY-memories. Or the Self Birth-Giver receives corrupted energy, and gives the received corrupted energy to corrupted beings if O is corrupted. O corruption adds up in the corrupted recoveries of Being, and diverts transmitters of Energy of Being further toward corruption, then ^{im}balance. ^{Im}balanced recoveries frustrate many Bodies, thus the Bodies succumb to accept that their Gain of Energy must be mixed with corruption. The transmitters eventually move toward the other end of the trade, and deliver Energy of Being modulated using terrorful carriers. This doesn't have to be the case, and can easily change if Selves seek TRANSPARENCY.

Regardless of the corrupted or TRANSPARENT or terrorful or LOVELY status of the Self Birth-Giver as a whole, till the end of Animation, the Self Birth-Giver will hold the power of command over all the Organizations of Animation regarding all of the desires of the Body. The collective of Self Birth-Givers dictate how bound Animation is desired, and who's desires are satisfied, and how desires are satisfied, and how O organizations must animate O desires.

Whether the Self Birth-Givers believe or not, deny or not, they manifest exactly how TRANSPARENT or corrupted, BALANCED or ^{im}balanced, LOVELY or terrorful the body-bound Animation losses or gains energy. The BALANCED Self Birth-Giver gives to BALANCED re-Birth. LOVELY; to LOVELY. corrupted; to corrupted.

The Birth-Giver animates all of Animation for Desire of Birth. The provided animation by Being is not bound to Selves, thus the animation can indeed suddenly end. The Birth-Giver does not need our consent to end the animation. And this animation is not perceived by the Body or Mind or Heart or Gut, either. Yet, there are no secrets that the Energy of the Birth-Giver flows through us.

Once we reach a point that BALANCE is impossible, Animation ends. However, the Creation that Being animates can cause far below impossible ^{im}balance, by design. Animation shuffles toward eventual BALANCE, if Animation has to. It is however best that, if the environment is ^{im}balanced, the Self Birth-Giver gives toward bringing ^{im}balance back to BALANCE.

The current Human knowledge of Being is limited to how the Body perceives Energy of Being and how the Self receives it. The desire of Human in understanding Energy of Being is not merely in the Body, but it has been perceived only that way. Thus, it has been difficult for Human to scientifically propose a purpose or desire for Human.

The Purpose is HEALTH. Desire is LOVE.

HEALTH is the giving Art of Man, his "trustworthy trinity": Birth, Justice, and Fate. Man gives Justice to whom needs it most, Being, the Core, Creator. Once Self TRANSPARENT: Body, Mind, re-Animation. LOVE is the giving Art of Woman, her "trustworthy trinity": Birth, Justice, and Fate. Woman gives Birth to whom needs it most, Being, the Core, Creator. Once Self TRANSPARENT: Body, Mind, re-Animation. Self TRANSPARENCY is key.

It is Fact that, without Loss of Generality, Man can be in the Body of Woman and Woman can be in the Body of Man and both can be in the BALANCED Body merely and simply if and only if not originating from Obsession and Compulsion.

The Unconscious Judge is the reason that the HEALTH of the Core can be perceived as $\equiv$ness, and the Self Birth-Giver is the cause of the terrorful recoveries of Energy bound to her time and place. The Unconscious Judge is the reason that HEALTH of the Core can be TRANSPARENTLY perceived and received without ^{im}balance, and the Self Birth-Giver is the cause of the LOVELY recoveries of Energy bound to her. The Unconscious Judge can cause Humanity HEALTHY, and the Birth-Giver can make Earth LOVELY. This is a matter of Faith.

Faith is reduced because of corruption; because the Self Birth-Giver is corrupted. O gives Birth to corrupted Unconscious Judges, and causes terrorful-memories in the form of misunderstood relationships.

When the Self Birth-Giver is corrupted, it operates exclusively on O most vulnerable bounds such as the physical, mental, and emotional body. O reacts strongly and potentially dangerously to all forms of Loss, and O reacts Self-Absorbedly to Gain.

Faith is restored by the TRANSPARENT BALANCED LOVELY Self Birth-Giver. O gives Birth to HEALTHY Unconscious Judges, and causes LOVELY-memories. O uses all TRANSPARENT BALANCED Points of Perception, and is driven by BALANCED recoveries.

It is not possible for the Self to skip directly to the state in which the corrupted Self Birth-Giver is made LOVELY, without all O TRANSPARENT receiving instruments in place. The corrupted Self Birth-Giver resists against TRANSPARENCY. O doesn't believe that O is corrupted, since O trusts only O-self perceptions of Body. Because, O pseudo-rationality convinces O that O perceptions come from the entire Being, and ☰-justifies that O-self perceptions of the Self-Body match with that of Being. The terrorful-memory of Body caused by trusting this pseudo-rationality must become TRANSPARENT.

Thus, the first line of Self Defense against corruption is the Rationality of the Self. The corrupted Self Birth-Giver receives corrupted recoveries of Energy. Strong TRANSPARENT BALANCED Rationality helps the Self Birth-Giver realize the fact that O Energy is corrupted. Thus the Self Birth-Giver strives toward TRANSPARENCY. Even though this does not mean that O becomes LOVELY, this is the first step. In Self Defense, the Rationality must be improved so that it becomes more powerful than the corrupted Self Birth-Giver. the Self, in this sense, can receive the cooperation of the Rest to become even exponentially more powerful than the corrupted Self Birth-Giver.

If the Self is influenced by any form of addiction or if the Rationality is ☰-employed as the force of the corrupted Self Birth-Giver, the corrupted Self Birth-Giver oversees all systems of the Self, and pursues the usage of the Body in any corrupted form that gives O the temporal gain of any Quantum. Regardless, Being animates all Selves, and being ends animation if it does not serve O desire toward the full spread of Birth.

So, it is best that even if the Body perceives an entire life of "enjoyable"[38] yet corrupted recovery of Energy, the Body TRANSPARENTLY animates BALANCED re-Birth.

When the Rationality of the Self is weak, the Self is influenced by the corrupted Body, corrupting the Self, and corrupting the Quantum of the Self, and adding the Self's Quantum to the corrupted recovery of Energy of the Rest. This is regardless of the physical attractiveness of the Body. The corrupted Body gives O Quantum to the next corrupted Body. The corrupted Quantum enters into the Body of the Rest, without knowledge and without consent. Of course, the corrupted Quantum is received by the Body because the Body seeks any gain of energy, whether the Quantum is TRANSPARENT or corrupted.

Once the corrupted Quantum enters the Body without knowledge and without consent, giving the Body the joyful gain of the Quantum (whose corruption remains naturally unperceived), the Body loads one of the most terrorful-memories that leads to lasting ⊟-conditioning in the Body's instruments, ⊟-intuitively perceiving corruption as pseudo-TRANSPARENCY. Thus the Body "believes" in corruption, and is convinced by pseudo-rationality that O is TRANSPARENT. Such a belief is reinforced further by the confirmation bias of the Body toward the joyful corrupted Quantum.

The Body is born LOVELY.

O has original LOVELY-memories, and O transmits these modulated LOVELY-memories outwardly. Even if the Body was once LOVELY, O can become unlovely. This happens because the load of LOVELY-memories have gradually faded, or made void or replaced by terrorful-memories caused by terrorful Quantums. The LOVELY-memories first become integrated, then unloaded. Then, the Body becomes loaded with terrorful-memories. These memories modulate themselves with the same carriers of LOVELY-memories. The Body, then, transmits the terrorful recoveries of the LOVELY-memories, which is to say that the Body's LOVELY-memories are made terror-integrated. In that situation things can get worse and worse. The worst:

---

38 ill-enjoyable

- Being within a corrupted terrorful environment. Happening today.

- The terrorful demodulators of the Self are trained to receive terrorful Quantums from Being and give them to the Body. Happening today.

- The ⇌ demodulators of the Unconscious are trained to give ⇌-Words to the Subconscious. Happening today.

- The terrorful Self-Conscious is not equipped with the knowledge of the process of connection to Being and communication with the Core.

- The Body is filled with terrorful-memories and shares these memories to the Rest. Happening today.

- The Subconscious is filled with ⇌-imprints and shares these imprints with the Rest. Happening today.

- The Self is in addiction. The Body perceptions are numbed. Happening.

- The flow of Energy is controlled by the corrupted Self Birth-Givers. Happening today.

- Power is given to organizations in support of corruption, ^{im}balance, ⇌ness, and terror. Happening today.

- The conscious is employed by the corrupted Self Birth-Giver and the Unconscious Judge. Everything is ⇌-justified and everyone is afraid. Happening today.

- The corrupted Self-Body transmits corrupted memories to the corrupted environment. Happening today.

- The corrupted environment transmits the corrupted memories of the Self to the Rest. Happening today.

An enormous amount of corruption, terror, ^{im}balance, and their terrorful-memories enter into the environment on many fronts, since no member of the corrupted environment have been careful to maintain TRANSPARENCY. This is a big loss.

Everything is animated by Being, and Being decides to end Animation if O doesn't fit in O Desire toward Birth. Being animates the entirely of Animation, so that Animation is eventually ended if O doesn't satisfy Being toward Birth. This is the Desire of Being. Thus it is best for the Self Birth-Giver to avoid this big loss, and to TRANSPARENTLY seek animation of the spread of BALANCED re-Birth. Through this process, O becomes LOVELY.

**BOUND ANIMATION HAS ACCESS TO
THE TRANSPARENT AND BALANCED
LOVELY BEING AND HEALTHY CORE.**

WHAT ANIMATION STANDS FOR

SELF-PRESERVATION

The timeline of Human began with tribes of extreme şåvågėry and tribes of extreme naivety, when the şåvågės repeatedly pushed the naive to extinction. Then, in their own selfish judgment, the şåvågės renamed the Word of "gėṅȯcįḍė" into the ⊟-invention of "Survival of the Fittest". By doing so, they redefined naturally BALANCED and LOVELY Human into naturally "competitive to death". And by the ⊟ness in their judgment, they assumed their victories by domination over others is blessed by some sort of god, which could be best recognized as the image of their own god-complex. Thus, they lived believing through the first common ⊟-imprint "The dead are evil, and the victorious are good", so that they hide under the protection of the çȯṙṙųᵽṫion of those who cause death.

The scriptures and history books written by the victors are evident that the victors have the future generations believe that this timeline of Human is simply a mix of arbitrary physical and mental battles of survival and the mere effects of Human "instinct". Bliss in their position (place) throughout all of this, their "instinct" is metamorphosed by the ⊟-imprint that speaks as "the blessed are victorious," while victory is a mere time-bound place-bound organization-bound bliss. The ⊟-imprint is caused by the çȯṙṙųᵽṫion of the HEALTHY-imprint that speaks as "The victorious are blessed" referring to those who conquer themselves toward TRANSPARENCY and thus are blessed to receive the BALANCE of the Core and Being.

All in all, what we are used to ⊟-call "creation" is able to adopt, and saves itself even if there is hardship and oppression and gėṅȯcįḍål attempts of the şåvågės, and even if there are natural extinctions, or successful attempts of the şåvågės at causing the extinction or severe injury of those who happen to be pretty naive in the middle of all of this. At any of the historically recorded attempts of the şåvågės at forcing the naive and unprepared others into extinction, some of the naive remained alive, and gave birth to their next generations. As they survived through hardship and oppression caused by the şåvågės, they learnt their lessons while maintaining their naive "belief" caused by the ⊟-imprint that speaks "humanity is naturally good". Thus, the instinct of the naive is that a day comes that things are made right.

Evidently, that requires a significant amount of patience. In reality, humanity is merely eventually good and is naturally inclined toward HEALTH[INESS] and LOVE[LINESS]. Man and Woman have proven repeatedly that they have special interests about HEALTH and LOVE, whether in the form of ⊟-Imprints or HEALTHY-imprints, terrorful-memories or LOVELY-memories. The Quantum is perceived by Man and Woman precisely the same.

Animation[39] as a whole inducts the same as the unbounded Naive. Animation invents many things in between the beginning and the end, not immediately observable by the bound Naive. Regardless, the Naive survives and is reborn as the inventor-for-all. The inventor-for-all invents for all of Animation. Whenever something is invented-for-all, the bound Animation expands in Being toward TRANSPARENCY, and the savagery of the collective all of Animation is reduced. As inventions-for-all continues, savagery approaches zero.

There has been many inventors-for-all in the past. To name a few, remember the inventor of a bowl to collect fluid water, a wheel to have a load run easier, and black powder for fireworks, but not black powder for canons. Sadness can be felt in history, being written by the ⊟-victorious who used black powder as "gun-powder". Gun-powder is just an invention-for-self.

The distinction between invention-for-all and invention-for-self is in what the invention stands for. The inventor-for-all stands for inventions that all of Animation stands for. While the inventor-for-self invents for what the bound Self stands for, whether the Self of an individual or the Self of an organization of Animation. It should be emphasized more, that once an invention-for-self is invented, it eventually becomes an invention-for-all, since if there is one thing worse than an invention-for-self, it is wasting an invention already invented. But, there exists still a key difference. An invention-for-self is originally intended merely for the self-bound Animation, while an invention-for-all is for all of Animation, as in, Animation stands for inventions-for-all without bounds such as self and time and place.

---

39 Unbound

The invention-for-all was known from the beginning to be. It is an extension of Creation, and thus a part of Creation. In other words, The invention-for-all of Animation is the Creation of Animation, and Animation stands for Creation. While an invention-for-self is just an invention.

The Creation of Animation is known by the Core from the beginning, while the inventions[-for-self] are not known by the Core. Being knows them, for Being contains them and Being knows the end. So even though the Creation of Animation was bound to the beginning, the inventions[-for-self] are the animation's choice.

The Creation of Animation, O inventions-for-all are bound from the beginning to be. The Creator knows. The Creator has no other choice but to create the Creation that O is bound to create. No matter how much O tries to avoid the eventuality of O Creation, O is forced to come back to it.

The end is in BALANCE, yet each and every invention[-for-self] and any invention of the animation in avoidance of O Creation alters the timelines of time-bound Animation, and alters the places of place-bound Animation (And so forth for all bounds), for the better or worse. This is the Free Will of Animation. You are free to invent.

If bound Animation becomes TRANSPARENT, O observes that O-self desires to employ O Free Will toward BALANCE thus LOVELINESS and HEALTHINESS. The Free Will is described in advanced sections of Coreology. Coreology is worthy to be deemed a creation destined to re-animate the time-bound animation as soon as possible toward the LOVE[LINESS] of Being "The Birth-Giver" and HEALTH[INESS] of the Core "The Judge". Coreology might be deemed a significant creation that gives this time-bound animation the knowledge of all of the tools that drive O timelines. This knowledge guides the Conscious, the Nonconscious, and the Body of this animation against corruption and toward TRANSPARENCY. At TRANSPARENCY, the Self preserves O TRANSPARENCY. Then, O is guided toward BALANCE. At BALANCE, O preserves O BALANCE. And O preserves HEALTH and LOVE, once O observes Animation in HEALTH and in LOVE.

SELF-MAINTAINABILITY

It might be known by now that the Core is so close O feels distant, is so observable that O feels overlooked, is so palpable that O feels neglected, and O delivers the Voice of the subjects of injustice so persistently that many prefer that O is not heard, and when O is heard the Voice is so loud it causes the corruption of pride.

At whichever the "correct" terminology is, the corruption must shift, turn, alter, get modified, transform, adjust, switch, convert, and/or evolve to TRANSPARENCY. The basic approach to be toward TRANSPARENCY in communication with the Core is acceptance of the need for self-maintenance. BALANCED and HEALTHY Animation stands for self-maintainability. This relies on the fact that, the recovery of the Message of the Core, the Word is uncodified and needs to be codified before rational understanding, and if the Word is codified with corruption, then [the codification] Algorithm, but not the uncodified Word, is buggy and must be fixed.

This is the matter of programming. When the Algorithm is buggy, it is debugged. This is what the Professional Programmer does.

The Professional Programmer does not insist on the name of the Core or the ⊟-imprint that speaks "My algorithm is perfect", but rather accepts that he/she can make errors, can cause bugs, and that he/she needs to maintain the Algorithm. He/she then either fixes his/her bugs, or if he/she is not a good programmer, he/she hires the Professional Programmer to fix him/her. A non-programmer should not insist that the Algorithm is correct, since he/she has zero understanding of programming let alone the one Algorithm.

For now, it suffices to say that the Professional Programmer does not accept the gibberish of the Words corruptly codified, but accepts that the codification Algorithm is buggy and needs to be debugged. the Professional Programmer does not believe that the Algorithm is absolutely bug-free and the resultant Words that has come from the Algorithm have always been TRANSPARENTLY codified. Pride appears since the originator of the original Algorithm was a very good programmer, so good that people called him "god".

The need for reduction of pride can be observed even more when the Professional Programmer realizes that the original code might have been re-programmed by many ⊟-imprints when no Conscious-Body was recording the ⊟ events in history.

the Professional Programmer solves problems, and as much as he/she should doubt himself/herself and consider that misunderstandings of the Words could potentially be his/her own "user error", he/she investigates how the Algorithm is precisely functioning, finds the bugs in it, reports the bugs, and fixes them.

The Professional Programmer does not try to justify the bugs and hide them under the rug. That's something lazy corrupted people do. the Professional Programmer diligently documents, reports, finds, and fixes the bugs.

While at it, the Professional Programmer back tracks the fixes in the Algorithm and finds the ⊟-Words of the original buggy algorithm, and corrects them too. the Professional Programmer does not blindly accept the old Words of the buggy Algorithm, instead re-performs tests and collects new Words from the fixed Algorithm.

The Professional Programmer knows, especially when it is about significant matters of life and death, it is not enough that the Algorithm just works or just works most of the times. He/she makes the Algorithm work all the time, since this Algorithm NEEDS to work all of the time. The Professional Programmer considers for all edge cases, and if there are bugs in the edge cases, they are also fixed. And if there remains Words that are not codified, or if their codification is corrupted whether partially or fully, the Professional Programmer corrects for that too.

The Professional programmer, specially and particularly, is not obsessed about his/her own modifications and inclusions of the Algorithm. He/she is not compelled to see them as his/her own "babies". The Professional Programmer treats his/her babies like they are the babies of anyone else. The Professional Programmer uses his/her good programming practices for his/her own babies like he/she does so for anybody's babies. And he/she does the same for himself/herself.

If there are certain conflicts in the provisions of Algorithm from one communion to the next, the Professional Programmer definitely does NOT kill or dream of killing other people's babies. Those are the two anti-Being anti-Core animations that corrupted imbalanced terrorful ☰ people do.

Finally, the Professional Programmer takes ownership and fixes his/her employer when the Algorithm is corrupted. And, if the Professional Programmer becomes an employee, he acts like a true leader, and creates Professional Programmers who are given the Free Will to fix the Algorithm when it is due.

SELF-CONFIDENCE

Once TRANSPARENT demodulation of the Message of the Core is done, there is the Word[40]. Then the Word is codified for consumption. But, then before it is shared, the Word is also encrypted, even though it does not have to be. It is clear that the Word has historically remained significantly mystical and encrypted. The secrets were historically not provided at ease. This is due to the being of oppression by corrupted environments who have constantly worked against the Deliverers [of the Word]. The mention of oppression is important since the ability to communicate with the Core most often relates to a catch 22. The catch 22 is that, the communication skills of the Deliverers are usually activated if and only if they suffer some form of Unconscious-opening oppression, usually involving some forms of false accusations. It is as if the oppressed are so silenced that they begin instead communicating with the Core to express their voice. That's perhaps one way, but still one forced way of discovering and practicing communication with the Core. But this practice doesn't have to be that way. And it is not the best way.

In times and places that are oppressive, the Deliverers deliver in imposed secrecy. Thus, they practically carry and deliver the Word mystically and encrypted. Due to existence of corruption, the Words become also ☰-imprinted. These ☰-imprinted mystical and encrypted Words, in absence of a proper science of the Core, are misinterpreted in many situations, in themselves causing more ☰-Words that cause further ☰-imprints that cause further ☰-Words. The environment and its members also living within its corruption are loaded with terrorful-memories. All the attempts of ☰-imprinted members at the decryption of the Words are also ☰-imprinted, and the ☰-imprinted decryptions of the ☰-Words are ☰-believed. The ☰-belief is not in the knowledge included in the Word, but rather in the Deliverers of the Word or the followers of the Deliverers and their Deliverers and their followers for many generations. While the knowledge is in the Word, and should not be ☰-judged by the knowledge of the Deliverer.

---

40   Just to avoid the confusion as it has come to Attention that some people may think that "the Word" is only one word, the Word is the reservoir that gives rise to each and every of many words.

In the middle of all of this, it has been very easy for some active ☰-advocates to pretend that some of their ☰-Words are "the messages of the Core" by associating their ☰-Words to the actual Deliverers. To make things more complicated, some incidental ☰-codifiers, regardless of their intentions, have ☰-codified the ☰-imprinted ☰-Words, became famous for it, and through that process caused ☰-imprints within various bounds of many organizations. The bound of time hasn't helped, and power-hungry individuals and organizations have used time, inventing more and more ^{im}balance in between individuals, organizations, and countries, and consequentially the bound Energy of Being. The gaps in people's lives are very noticeable and considerable.

Considering these issues which are TRANSPARENT to the unbound animation, the Self needs confidence to reach the state of BALANCE. The BALANCED confident Self only assumes that beliefs are not necessarily the way they are presented in this ^{im}balanced recovery filled with ☰-imprints and terrorful-memories. He/she has faith, and through faith, he/she recognizes corruption and diagnoses ☰ness, with an extra-ordinary amount of due diligence, brings TRANSPARENCY forward, and provides HEALTH and LOVE for the betterment of all of the animation. Animation stands for such self-confidence.

SELF-MUTABILITY

Human once believed that elements of life are magical. Fire was dangerous, and water was uncontrollable, soil was wild, and metal was unmanageable. The understanding of elements was so crude that Human "believed" that they were created by some extreme being, and they coul be controlled only by some form of extremism. Laws were established accordingly. But, then someone mutated, altered the Law in everyone's Body-Conscious. The mutated thus invented a new Law, either for all or for self. The HEALTHY-mutated tamed fire and water and soil and metal for the comfort of all. The ☰-mutated invented-for-self the "ownership" of the material whose original owner was Being, and used the elements of life as weapons. The examples of such mutations are plenty. And as such, with HEALTHY mutability, creativity grows. The bound animation as a whole created many forms of science and art, by the HEALTHY mutated Selves.

Healthy mutation is the Form of HEALTHY protest. HEALTHY self-mutation is the Self's Desire to be a unique Gene, entirely mono and new, in protest against the overreaching ☰ness and the mutations of it.

Many selves invented, using the Free Will, but mostly to eliminate fair competition, not to embrace it. The savages used the elements, not as a tool to invent-for-all but, to invent-for-self methods of theft from the Rest, whether lives, bodies, or other resources. The savages used water as trap, carbon to poison, democracy to dictate, God to control, and science for weapons of mass-murder.

It is clear that there are many critical ☰nesses and many small ones in the current operation of the self-bound animation, needless to say that the members of the animation range still from savage to naive, operator to programmer, inventor to creator, consumer to producer, agents of balance to ^{im}balance, and many other categories. It is important to bring this animation back to HEALTH, especially when these ☰nesses hold the animation's way of embodied consciousness hostage upon all the most sensitive organs of the Body so tightly that the animation cannot free O-self away. It is clear that this animation holds wrong belief systems, caused by these ☰nesses.

The s̲a̲v̲a̲g̲e̲s̲ once believed the left-handed are evil, sexually-active women are witches, the sun evolves around the Earth. One may think that after the discovery of all those mistakes, their most recent civilization has learnt a few lessons and would treat the world better, but it only got worse. They didn't learn anything from the past. Small particles were divided by science while the s̲a̲v̲a̲g̲e̲s̲ ate, even up to very recently, the mummified flesh of their arch-nemesis. Thinking of nothing but "winning", the s̲a̲v̲a̲g̲e̲s̲ have mastered the manufacturing of w̲e̲a̲p̲o̲n̲s̲ of mass-destruction, reached no BALANCED peaceful conclusion, and are doing even worse than the entirety of their past history combined. They merely got more ☴-civilized at hiding their ☴-traces using the technologies of c̲o̲r̲r̲u̲p̲t̲i̲o̲n̲.

For the most of the history, the s̲a̲v̲a̲g̲e̲s̲ have made the naive extincted. But, at least, at old times, their brain was small. What is the excuse for the p̲s̲e̲u̲d̲o̲-rationality of today? The average person is desensitized, the scientists are bought, the judges are limited, the lawyers care only for money. One half ☴-believes that "it is what it is", and the other half ☴-believes that "is not in control". The philosophers and the clergy of the s̲a̲v̲a̲g̲e̲s̲ have assumed that the entire animation is "evil" so that they can deflect their own evilness to the entirety of Animation, inventing the ☴-print that speaks as "Human is naturally evil" employing which most of the citizens of s̲a̲v̲a̲g̲e̲ nations p̲s̲e̲u̲d̲o̲-rationalize. The survived naive remained and secretly whispered it how it is in this HEALTHY-imprint:

Bound Animation expands by BALANCE.

Instead, the s̲a̲v̲a̲g̲e̲s̲ believe that mass-m̲u̲r̲d̲e̲r̲ of the children of the Rest must be normalized. For thousands of years, the s̲a̲v̲a̲g̲e̲s̲ have told each other about their daydreams and scripted their daydreams into stories about having the children of their arch-nemesis die in one way or another. Even at the most vulnerable positions, the s̲a̲v̲a̲g̲e̲ p̲s̲e̲u̲d̲o̲-rational mind asked his/her god to kill the children of their enemies. It is not possible to distinguish in between rationality and p̲s̲e̲u̲d̲o̲-rationality by the math and logic, but it is possible to recognize the s̲a̲v̲a̲g̲e̲ p̲s̲e̲u̲d̲o̲-rational mind through such dreams and such requests from his/her god. Their god is clearly not the Core. Such ☴-dreams and ☴-prayers and ☴-actions against Children is in severe conflict with a major and never-changing HEALTHY-imprint:

CHILDREN ARE LOVELY.

SELF-RELIANCE

For all that is said so far, it is important, thus, to have ⊟-imprints become TRANSPARENT, and to recover the HEALTHY-imprints. Coreology re-evaluates the instruments of Animation regarding the process of demodulation of the Message of the Core, codification of the resultant Word, demodulation of the Energy of Being, and codification of the resultant Quantum. This enables this bound animation toward BALANCE.

pseudo-rational Animation tends to deny the being of the complete[d bound] Conscious and tends to ⊟-justify that "invention-for-all does not exist and everything is pure competition". Organizations, once in domination over the Rest, assume that whatever is, it is what it is and that's all there is to it. Coreology is critical of such ⊟-assumptions and is able to present the fact that bound Animation always has at least the one Conscious rational enough to create BALANCE for the entirety of this animation, and that this animation must rely on O-self to reach BALANCE.

Before everyone is on board, some resilient ⊟-imprints must become TRANSPARENT. The most elder ⊟-imprints that have long lived for thousands of years are hard to become TRANSPARENT. The complex reason for this is the fact that the organizations who benefit from these long-lived ⊟-imprints believe that "Those who are dead are evil, and those who are victorious are good" and that "The imprints that have vanished must have been ⊟, and the imprints that remain must be HEALTHY". It is ironic that "The complex reason that these ⊟-imprints remain" is that the reason for these ⊟-imprints are themselves: They are self-fulfilling prophecies, consistent imprints of confirmation bias powered by the desire of ⊟ness to cause the death of the HEALTHY. ⊟ness kills HEALTH as if HEALTH never existed, so HEALTHINESS cures ⊟ness so ⊟ness ceases to exists. The end result of the two sounds the same, but the two are different.

There is a difference between HEALTHY desire and ⊟ desire. The latter is the cause of ⊟-imprints and ⊟-Words in which the symptoms of ⊟ness such as weakness and death are ⊟-assumed to be the symptoms of the "wrath of god".

HEALTHY desire is of two main types:

1) The desire to cause HEALTHINESS for the betterment of all.

2) The desire to cause HEALTHINESS for the betterment of self[41].

The Selves striving toward the first type genuinely cause HEALTHY Words and imprints, at least for the amount applicable to the practical bound knowledge of their time, space, Body, Conscious, Nonconscious, Birth and Death. These Selves genuinely have these HEALTHY Words and imprints heard, acknowledged, and welcomed for the betterment of all.

The Selves striving toward the second type may do so due to survival, which is given and must be. It is also TRANSPARENT that there is a move toward balance if the Self strives toward implanting HEALTHY-imprints and uttering HEALTHY Words. However, it is a selfish move (and not necessary toward the betterment of all) if the Self does so for maximized convenience of the Self or for the want of the maximum survival of the Self's such legacies as last name, race, or nation.

God gives to any Human that asks, whether they are seeking BALANCE or imbalance. It is an imperative HEALTHY-imprint to not lose hope merely because of the existence of the ☰-imprint that speaks as "The winners are blessed by God." This ☰-print is the farthest from fact. Everybody and everyone is absolutely equitably blessed by God. If a blessing is not equitable, you would know that it is not the blessing of God. The rest of "blessings" come from bound yet powerful quasi-secret organizations in the business of ☰-Words that sound somewhat pseudo-rationally reasonable. These organizations invent imbalance, are ☰, cause ☰-imprints, and then rely on their own self-caused ☰-imprints to justify their blessings.

Typically, the organizations that rely on such ☰-imprints are the ones on the dominant side of the existing imbalance, thus they desire imbalance, and perform any action to control and dominate the rest of organizations [and selves] through their ☰ desire to control the flow

---

41 Whether Selves or Organizations

of the Message of the Core[42]. Control of the Core[43] leads to the collective manifestation of the desires of the dominant. It must be apparent that the desire to control the Core, which roots and results in the Control of the Rest of the Selves, is done with ⊟-intentions.

Yet, in rare cases, a HEALTHY leader desires to control the flow of the Message of the Core in order to control the Rest of the Selves toward TRANSPARENCY, BALANCE, and thus HEALTH. And in such rare cases, as the Will of the Core and the Will of the leader are aligned, the implicit Control of and by the Core becomes possible. This Control by the Core leads to the same collective manifestation of desires, but that of the leader aligned with the Core, of eventual HEALTH. This is done for HEALTHY intentions, and it is significantly hard to do.

The elder ⊟-imprint that speaks as "The winners are blessed by God." has lived for too long. It is difficult to make it TRANSPARENT. The self-fulfilling prophecy is at hand, strong. The winners dominate, and in their authority, they have no reason to believe that winners are not blessed by God, and they would justify anything with their pseudo-rationality to keep things the way they are. This is partly due to the fact that sometimes the victory of winners is indeed blessed by God. So how can the type of victory be distinguished? It was already explained before. To reiterate, simply put and at the expense of causation of potential justifications, just consider being a professional detective. To find the murderer, trace the motivation.

As difficult as it may seem, Self-bound Animation can rely on O-self to know the answer. If it seems difficult to know the answer, it is because the Self-bound animation does not want to know the answer. And perhaps the reason for that is, the dominant Selves and Organizations of this animation are corrupted, imbalanced, ⊟, and/or terrorful. As the animation expands, O will eventually know. And, O will, by Self-Reliance. Animation of Domination by ⊟ness is liable for all damages to people, including but not limited to corruptive, imbalancing, terrorful, and/or ⊟ness causing damages.

---

42 For short called, Control of the Core
43 As eventually futile of an effort Control of the Core is, since it is, not the Core but, the Rest which is controlled

SELF-DEFENSE

There is a vast difference between the Animation of Domination by ≣ness (AODI) and the Animation of Leadership by the Core (AOLC), regardless of the fact that AODI is intelligent about the simple deceptive fact that they should pretend to be "leaders", they should be politically correct, and pretend that they dominate only for falsified yet good reasons. It is possible to p̃sẽũdõ-rationally justify for almost anything, but transactions cannot be faked. Thus, to be the Professional Detective, trace the transactions.

AODI's game is not fair. O uses any form of power to expand in dominance, and to shrink AOLC. AODI uses ≣-recoveries of HEALTHY Words, and keeps O ≣ness c̃õr̃r̃ũp̃tly secret and classified. AODI then falsely accuses AOLC by labeling them with ≣-Words, causing many Selves to ≣-perceive AOLC as ≣. Of course, the organizations of AOLC, from the smallest atoms to its members and expanded larger organizations, always possess some weaknesses. AODI uses these weaknesses to justify for O false accusations against AOLC. The Professional Detective, thus firstly, should not assume that the entirety of AOLC is ≣ if some members of O have conceived some ≣ness. AODI being far from perfect, The Professional Detective should secondly not assume that AOLC must be perfect. These two are the things that a c̃õr̃r̃ũp̃ted ^im balance ≣ terrorful member of AODI does through O justifications by p̃sẽũdõ-rationality.

The HEALTHY AOLC, as weak as O body may be within the dominance of AODI, must play a different game. AOLC implants the bound animation with HEALTHY-imprints and seeks to enforce Acceptance of BALANCE, against all odds. AODI, holding strong within their dominance, implants the animation, especially their own organizations and members, with ≣-imprints and terrorful-memories funded by AODI and falsely associated with AOLC.

AODI pretends that O ≣ness is the desire of the entirety of Animation, effectively rebranding AODI ≣nesses as p̃sẽũdõ-AOLC healthiness, and AOLC HEALTHINESS as ≣ness.

AODI fools O own members into believing O, and the members do not seem to include the HEALTHY instruments that can help them identify the ^{im}balanced ⊟ situation, or find themselves hopeless in causing change, and thus accept yet one of the other powerful ⊟-imprints of AODI whose members repeat: "I am not in Control".

AOLC seeks HEALTHY Leadership that can provide the members of AODI with the Control they want to have, but AOLC is falsely accused by AODI. Even if AOLC earns Leadership, AOLC earns it with hardship and inherits only an ^{im}balanced terrorful recovery of Energy, as AODI clings to O Domination to the last breath. Many would be upset at AOLC, if AODI loses power, because AOLC does not seek to steal from others to give to O-self like how AODI animates. But if there is patience, all of that hardship goes away and will be realized as temporary.

AOLC would need to correct for a massively damaged bound Animation. The work of AOLC begins, not only after O gains and earns Leadership but, mostly during the Domination of AODI. AOLC should and must actively:

- Make AODI ⊟-imprints TRANSPARENT, and eventually recovered back to their original HEALTHY-imprint.

- Enhance existing HEALTHY-imprints by TRANSPARENCY and practicality toward complete HEALTHINESS.

- Defend the Selves who need to survive

- Defend the Selves who push ^{im}balance back to BALANCE

- Defend the Selves who want to enable HEALTH

- Defend the Selves who want to enable LOVE

- Resist against losing leadership

- Resist flowing with the dominant recovery of Energy

- Defend TRANSPARENCY against corruption

- Teach the Selves to TRANSPARENTLY communicate with the Core

- Teach the Selves to receive the TRANSPARENT BALANCED recovery of Energy

- Enable the Selves toward TRANSPARENCY, BALANCE, HEALTH, and LOVE

It is difficult for unsupported Selves, without AOLC, to know how to reach these states by themselves. The ⊟-Words in the games and dances of AODI, and O music and media and books and concerts and comedy and nightlife weighs heavily on the entirety of bound Animation, but AOLC knows that O stops when O work is done. Unlike AODI which uses any opportunity to hypnotize the bound Animation including O own members, AOLC defends the Selves by reminding them of the HEALTHY-imprints that has always been within them through the Core, and teaches the Selves to create LOVELY-memories through Being. Every Self has this defense mechanism in them since the beginning. The TRANSPARENT BALANCED Self stands for self-defense.

Perhaps the only system under AODI that still strives toward BALANCED HEALTH is the judicial system of AODI. Perhaps, that is why that AODI's judicial system remains hated and underfunded. Even though many of the judges of the judicial system of AODI strive toward BALANCED HEALTH, many of the staff of this system are employed by ⊟ lobbyists. The judicial system of AODI needs the help of AOLC to recover the TRANSPARENT BALANCED HEALTHY Quantums and Words. AOLC should fully cooperate with the BALANCED judges within the system of AODI toward that goal.

SELF-SOBRIETY

It is unfortunate that many languages are bound to train the Body-Conscious, since Birth, to use proper nouns. The ⊟ Encryption of the Word in such languages is the main cause of the invention of ⊟-imprints presenting themselves in corrupted forms of nouns, designations, symbols, labels, titles, names, identifiers, idols and signs, and stars.

It is imperative to understand that the Message, and its TRANSPARENTLY demodulated Word, and its HEALTHY-imprints can neither be cloned nor rephrased. Thus, ⊟-imprinted HEALTHY-imprints must be cryptographically re-discovered, or in other words, re-encrypted-re-decrypted, by TRANSPARENT BALANCED HEALTHY means. This is done through Coreology. Simply put, ⊟-imprints are made TRANSPARENT through re-animation. Once ⊟-imprints of the Conscious and the Nonconscious are made TRANSPARENT, the Core is made observable, and the Message is TRANSPARENTLY demodulated and codified.

As AOLC's come and go, their followers may not get fully extincted by AODI's. The purpose of these followers is, not to clone the Word delivered by AOLC but, to believe and to have faith that it is POSSIBLE to TRANSPARENTLY receive and TRANSPARENTLY decrypt in BALANCE. The best teacher does not show you how it is done, but shows you that it can be done. Once you believe that it can be done, you can do it. ⟨Revelation⟩ does not lie in the Message, but in the fact that the Message exists. It is proven that the Message exists, even though clearly the proof of its existence has not been "good" enough for everyone, since its demodulation and codification and cryptography have not been entirety TRANSPARENT and BALANCED.

HEALTHY-imprints turn into ⊟-imprints due to ⊟-use and abuse, ⊟-programming practices, pure ⊟-desire of some organizations toward implanting ⊟-imprints, and many more ⊟-causes. Many ⊟-imprints censor HEALTHY-imprints by associating their own ⊟ to HEALTHINESS, and thus, they corrupt HEALTHY-imprints. There is apparently no lack of reasons for some Selves to desire corruption.

Thus, it is best if the followers of AOLC learn how to, themselves, receive the Message of the Core, rather than fully relying on the existing ⊟-imprinted recoveries of the Word, the recovery of the Message. It is not HEALTHY to be drunk on corruption, whether it comes from the corruption of AODI or the corruption of AOLC. It is not good to be drunk on the desires of excessive Selves, but it is not best either to be drunk on two-thousand-year-old wine, even though the knowledge of existence of the wine is well-appreciated.

With the help of Coreology, once enough Selves of Animation bring TRANSPARENCY and BALANCE to the Nonconscious, HEALTH[INESS] of the Core to the Nonconscious; Once the Conscious observes the HEALTH[INESS] of the Core, then science finds the proof it requires about the HEALTHY existence of the Core.

Currently, ⊟-imprints are dominant, AODI is Authority, O corrupted Conscious pseudo-rationally declares O-self victorious, blessed by God, not to be questioned, always right, while O-self carelessly seeks the desires of the Body, and crushes any competition economically, if not possible, by pseudo-justified bullying labeled war. AODI, having the most of the bound knowledge, and controlling the flow of information, ⊟-believes that O possesses the complete[d bound] knowledge. O ⊟-feels being "blessed" in the Body. O must be obeyed, or else all options are on the table. O does anything to hold onto power and domination, while O animates ill-imprints by O superiority-complex and images low of the Rest.

AODI believes that "If we lose Domination to another organization, the other organization treats us with the same corruption as we have treated them" This ⊟-imprint, as modern as it is, is also very hard to kill, because it appeals to an imaginary consequence caused by the intrinsic ⊟-intentions of AODI O-self.

AODI does not understand that if O acknowledges O ⊟ness and voluntarily gives the ⊟ness up, AOLC is always ready to forgive and help AODI back to HEALTHINESS.

AOLC has made it abundantly TRANSPARENT that they train their members for forgiveness. AODI is blind to this fact. It is clear that AODI is drunk and is the low of this animation while O ⊟-believes in that O is the high.

It is Fact that the Rest of this animation possesses more HEALTHY-imprints and less ⊟-imprints and would be more forgiving if AODI voluntarily gives up their Dominance to the Rest, which clearly seeks more BALANCE than AODI.

AODI, however, is a fool and thus will never consider voluntarily stepping down. Nobody has more ⊟-motivation toward corrupted ^{im}balance than AODI. If that was not true, AODI would have not been the pioneer in the ^{im}balance of O Domination.

AODI thus continues on the path of being drunk on the power of O Domination, and pseudo-rationally justifies that tens of nations with total population of hundreds of millions of LOVELY and HEALTHY "The Rest are demons, and animals, and terrorists, and barbarians..."

AODI sanctifies the actions of Some Name by reliance on the sanctified usage of the Some Name in ⊟-imprinted recoveries of the Message of God, because O is drunk on names.

Once a glorified communion of God is satisfied that Some Name is holy and protected, they implant the ⊟-imprints of the Some Name on themselves. As such, it becomes so easy for Some State of AODI to adopt the Some Name as the Name of the Some State, performing any atrocity in the name of the Some Name and getting away with it, since the glorified communion of God is disabled about fighting against the ⊟-use of the Some Name in any shape or form and is thus practically fully silenced and oppressed. This silence/oppression is however Self-Imposed.

It is best that such communions become sober by ceasing the Self-Imposition of their silence, and be TRANSPARENT and declare that even though the Some Name is holy, its usage is being extremely unholy, and make it TRANSPARENT that the "enemies" of the Some corrupted State of the Some Name are but humans who are going through significant Loss one after another generation.

Extreme reactions of a few of the Rest of humans does not represent the HEALTH[INESS] and LOVE[LINESS] of the Rest. The Rest are HEALTHY AND LOVELY, and they do not deserve to be treated any less than Human. Any rational human agrees.

Of course the Rest are LOVELY AND HEALTHY. Thus AODI uses lots of Energy to maintain O pseudo-rationality of reducing the Rest so that O maintains O Dominance over them. Have all of that energy been used not as such, the world was in a much better place.

To maintain power, AODI needs to manufacture weapons. To maintain O pseudo-rationality, AODI needs to retain secret and classified information or otherwise has O security wither in full TRANSPARENCY. To succeed, AODI relies on ☰-imprinted "words" and "messages" of attractive entities such as God, Democracy, Love, and Freedom, thus relies on corruption in the name of these entities. If the corruption is gone, AODI is at risk, so AODI makes sure O own members remain corrupted and pseudo-rational. As a matter of fact, this conclusion runs both ways. If and only if AODI relies on ☰-imprinted messages of God and relies on corruption to succeed, then O needs to classify information or otherwise has O security wither in full TRANSPARENCY. Through investigations of this two-directional condition, the Rest succeeds in recognizing who are the AODI and in eventually bringing AODI back to BALANCE and TRANSPARENCY. This is not too difficult.

All that AODI has in O defense arsenal is offensive weapons of mass-murder and mass-theft. This is easily recognizable. Their income depends on it, and the transactions are TRANSPARENT. Everybody knows who is in the business of selling weapons. AODI contains a legal system that plays with words. This is easily recognizable. AODI is able to hold onto agreements so long as they benefit O and is able to breach them when they don't benefit O. This ability is acknowledged.

Ironically, AODI ☰-believes that O is rational, but within O justified pseudo-rationality, O has concluded that O should hold onto O Dominance by any means, including mass-murder and mass-theft and the sales of weapons. This pseudo-rationality exists because O possesses yet another complex set of ☰-imprints that say "The other race is irrational. If our rational race does not dominate the other race, then they will irrationally dominate us." It is not too difficult to notice that these imprints are caused by being drunk on power, not by rationality.

AODI, admittedly, is more intelligent, but in their intelligence lies their brutal cruelty in the form of p̃šẽũd̃õ-rationality. If the naive someday lose all of their naivety, they may as well notice that the members of AODI have brutally m̃ũr̃d̃er̃ed their own communication with the Core so much that O has turned Nonconsciously insane and Consciously so intelligent yet p̃šẽũd̃õ-rational that O can justify anything. They want to love, but can only imitate it p̃šẽũd̃õ-rationally and that makes their Nonconscious insanely envious of the Rest who are capable of true LOVE. AODI pushes O insane p̃šẽũd̃õ-rationality to the point that AODI wants to paint the Rest of Animation as demons, so that AODI doesn't feel deviated from the self-deception that they are capable of loving their enemies.

In truth, Animation seeks only the Core, and will eventually become TRANSPARENT through the Core. Thus, without being BALANCED and without receiving the HEALTH[INESS] of the Core, TRANSPARENT Animation knows that O cannot truly receive LOVE[LINESS] from Being. This is the Rationality of a sober Animation. It is best if AODI realizes this and returns to the Core, Auto-returner Auto-Comer. It is time for the drunk by power to become sober.

Regardless, there is hope. AOLC is still in O right place in the Core, and will no-doubt remain and eventually be in Leadership. The first thing that Coreology knows about AOLC is that O is forgiving. Even if AODI killed their own communication with the Core permanently, if AODI acknowledges their ⊟ness, then AOLC wills to enable AODI to TRANSPARENCY, as difficult of a task it is, if not entirely too late. Of course, AODI must desire to be TRANSPARENT. AOLC can observe AODI until the cause of O ⊟-imprints are observed and re-animated, and the ⊟-imprints are made TRANSPARENT. AODI then reaches the revelation that the Core is observable, then AOLC helps training AODI to revive O instruments of communication with the core and TRANSPARENTLY demodulate the Message of the Core. Then, AOLC trains AODI using HEALTHY-imprints as deep as AODI desires through re-animation of what AODI has done to the Rest.

SELF-RECOVERY

As early as 5000 years before Christ, the TRANSPARENT Human has known and appreciated the Core. Then the Core became generally unobservable due to significant ⊟ness and corruption. The Core came back strongly observable around 1500-500 before Christ, but not heavily in majority of individuals. Then, AOLC studied Coreology and cured many of AODI of their times using it. at various times in history at multiple occasions, Coreology was re-discovered re-provided, but then suppressed by AODI who oppressed AOLC.

In the times of oppression, the oppressors made any attempt at nullifying the HEALTH[INESS] of the codified unencrypted knowledge of Coreology where ever found. They destroyed the TRANSPARENTLY demodulated and codified [unencrypted] Message of the Core, or they implanted ⊟-imprint into Coreology to justify their own corrupted narratives. They burnt all the books of Coreology, and killed whoever wrote them or read them or whoever memorized the content. By employing their pseudo-rationality, the oppressors ⊟-believed that they burnt the books of demons and the blasphemous, while they themselves were the ⊟ ones. Regardless, some written knowledge of Coreology remained. As a matter of fact, all that is needed to remain remained.

The oppressed knew that the oppressors would do the above mentioned atrocities, so the oppressed came up with smart plans to save Coreology for later generations. The oppressed wrote down Coreology in encrypted language, knowing that the encryption saves the writings of Coreology from extinction, and knowing that all of its encrypted language will be recovered in the far future when Cryptography of Coreology is fully codified, and Information Theory is fully decrypted.

The oppressed wrote down Coreology in the form of beautiful mystery, prose, poetry, drama, and many other forms of art. They adorned the knowledge with visual and sonic arts in the form of music and performance. Even though they knew that their flesh does not remain, they knew that their beautifully encrypted knowledge of Coreology remains protected. AODI couldn't detect them. Even if AODI recognized the Deliverers of the knowledge, AODI could not resist enjoying the beauty of AOLC knowledge. And so remained some of the Coreology material: The beautifully encrypted ones. Not only these materials remained hidden from AODI for thousands of years, they were so beautiful that AODI O-self became the entity preserving them, without knowing that they are Coreology materials. This process has continued till today by many creators of Art. These materials are the advanced knowledge of Coreology, and they already exist, even thought they are encrypted.

Thus, it is important to understand that all the present attempts at recovering some knowledge of Coreology is only at the level of recovering the basics of Coreology, the part that was burnt by AODI. The advanced material are already contained in the rest of literature, in beautifully encrypted form. The Art of the Word, in whichever form it is from poetry to prose and essay and comedy, proves the HEALTH[INESS] of the Core, and the Artist [of the Word] delivers the encrypted Word.

Even though not all of the artists who invent art invent it for all, there are many Artists who invent-for-all Art thus create the Art. Even though these Artists are a small percentage of the inventors of all art, and even though a small percentage of art is the Art of the Word, there still exists out there a significant amount of the Art, in various forms. It is possible to find the Poetry of the Core. It is possible to find the Prose of the Core. It is possible to find the HEALTHY mystical recoveries of the encrypted Word of the Core.

Contrary to the current common belief, science also works toward the recognition of the Core. science is provided. Indeed science is the strongest instrument for the recovery of Energy of Being and the Message of the Core, O best instrument of Cryptography and Information Theory. From the beginning, science willed to be the weapon of the Core against AODI. As soon as scientists are not inclined to align their results with their AODI fundraisers, science earns its position as the weapon of the Core. The case of science is curious. Each and every thing in science has been manifested by the Mind, thus each and every thing in science applies to the Mind. Science is the invention of the Mind for the discovery of bound Animation, and it will one day be for the discovery of the entirety of Animation. It is possible to recover science as the weapon of the Core.

Many parts of the advanced knowledge of Coreology is provided in the past by Selves of AOLC. It is possible to recognize and re-discover them by searching for the Style of the Core. The Style is described in another writing, but it can be found everywhere, and it is in every language. Yet, It is still easier to develop HEALTHY-imprints by reading and listening and writing and speaking in languages of cultures where people have spent thousands of years doing nothing but developing the Art of the Word. Persian, Aramaic, Sanskrit, Greek, Tamil, and Sumerian are perhaps filled with the Art. These are the advanced materials of Coreology, and are fully decryptable.

Even though codifying languages like English are not very compatible with adopting the proper decryption of the encrypted knowledge of the Core, and cannot properly codify the Art of the Word, the TRANSPARENT interpretations of the Art to English is possible. Regardless, the basics of Coreology are being made available in English and can be made available in any Language by TRANSPARENT translators. The English language is designed to be a good codifier, so it suits the basics of Coreology. Coreology must be practiced by ^{im}balanced humans. They can become TRANSPARENT thus BALANCED thus HEALTHY.

It is easy to apply the habits and processes of Coreology, and anyone can assist their friends and family in their path toward TRANSPARENCY. Once the basics of Coreology is established, there exists the entirety of the path from fully ^{im}balanced to fully BALANCED thus LOVELY and HEALTHY. Even reaching from fully-^{im}balanced to medium TRANSPARENCY is a step big enough for many in their entire lifetime.

Coreology answers, with the HEALTHY definiteness of the Core, any questions that a BALANCED human needs to know about. Thus, ⇌ness can be vanished. Safety in embrace of the Core can be felt. It will be known that the Core accepts all inclinations and desires of the Self so long as they do not lead Being toward corruption and ^{im}balance. It will be known that any form of energy can be used as a tool causing further BALANCE. The approach of Human toward Being will be advanced, and LOVE of Human toward Being; Real, Passion; BALANCED, Care; BALANCED, Human Rights; BALANCED, Quality; BALANCED, and even financial motivation; BALANCED.

Coreology is the Law since the beginning because the Core is the knowledge of the beginning, and Coreology is the study of the Core. Coreology has been established many times in many languages, even though its written decryptions has been burnt down by many powerful AODI's. And no matter how many times its written decryptions are burnt down, it is the Phoenix always reborn from the ashes, since the Core exists and is identical in all humans, whether they like it or not, or TRANSPARENTLY communicate with O or not, since the Core is the Identical Infinitesimal.

Coreology applies to all humans, and the Core gives to all humans without exception, needless to say that the Core gives to each in their own circumstances. The Core doesn't change, even though the perception of O and the demodulation of the Message of O thus the codified recovery of the Word can possess so much variety of 🗐-imprints and lack of transparency that it makes humans suspect that O is identical or even existing. The Core nevertheless is and is never-changing, and the study of the Core never dies. The First Law of Coreology is simple and consistent.

The entirety of Animation is recorded by the Core.

Thus the records of Animation are always recoverable. the Nonconscious can receive the Message of the Core, and demodulate it to the Word. The recovery of the Word is in the form of re-Animation, as Animation is recorded in the core and is played back exactly as it is.

The Second Law is the same.

Bound Animation is bound to re-Animation of the entirety of Animation.

It is to say that, if such bounds as time and place are released, the knowledge of Animation is completely shared. Whether or not bound Animation resists re-animating Animation, O is bound to re-animate in one way or another. And the more O resists, O is bound to suffer more from being bound to it. The more O suffers the more O implants 🗐-imprints on O. This gets more and more difficult, but regardless, this animation is bound to re-animate the entirety of Animation.

It is best to re-animate every animation as soon as possible. It is possible to do so with minimum Loss of Energy.

- First, the animation desires to have O ⊟-imprints made TRANSPARENT.

- To make the imprints TRANSPARENT, the cause of the imprints must be re-animated. Re-animation of the cause of HEALTHY-imprints is welcoming. That of ⊟-imprints is resistive.

- the Self re-animates the causes of all O imprints. The Body; O. The Conscious; O. The Subconscious; O. The Unconscious; O.

- The Self, The Body, The Conscious, the Subconscious, the Unconscious become TRANSPARENT.

The Nonconscious can receive and demodulate the Message of the Core. The Core records all of Animation, and the Message of the Core is the animation. Thus the Unconscious' recovery of the Message is the process of re-animation. The resultant Word makes the ⊟-imprints lose their ⊟ness and turn into void-imprints.

This work must be done until all imprints are made void, including the most root original imprint. Once the Self accepts all re-animation, this original imprint is void. At this point all of the imprints become void. Then, the Self is in BALANCE. This does not mean yet that the imprints are HEALTHY. It means that once all imprints are Void, the Core is observable. The Self is open and can welcome HEALTH.

- Once the Core is observable, the core trains the instruments of the Nonconscious.

- The instruments learn to TRANSPARENTLY demodulate and codify the Message of the Core, TRANSPARENTLY recovering the Word.

- This Word causes HEALTHY-imprints to appear in the Nonconscious.

- HEALTHINESS replace the void of void-imprints.

- HEALTHY-imprints are placed further in the Nonconscious.

- The Nonconscious is driven toward being HEALTHY. A symptom of this is that the Self gives O will to the service of the Core, finding HEALTH, and wishes to deliver the Message to the Selves of the Rest.

- Thus the Self recovers.

In the end, with the help of Coreology, the habits leading to TRANSPARENT, BALANCED, and eventually HEALTHY recovery can be understood and can be applied by any average people, granted that they are willing. Quick recovery approaches or long term habits exists for beginners to professionals who want to test themselves toward Coreology. There will be instructions. No specific background is needed. All the work of Cryptography is codified, and Information Theory is decryped. At the most basic level, this will enable you to eliminate ⊟nesses from which you are made to suffer against your will and your capacity for personal happiness increases. At the same basic level if applied to the entire society, happiness increases. This same basic level of Coreology operates much better than any form of healing or therapy available out there, and can be used in groups or as the best tool for self-improvement and self-recovery.

In the advanced levels, Coreology creates LOVE and HEALTH in many forms such as harmony and peace, and it will lead to justice, equity, and beauty on Earth as soon as possible, even though these are the eventual reality regardless. And those who cause ⊟-animation and resist re-animating the animations of ⊟ness will re-animate the animations of all ⊟, regardless, eventually. We are all in this together. Animation stands for self-recovery.

SELF-TESTABILITY

A fundamental ⊟ness is the inclination of the self-bound Animation[44] toward learning merely through the Conscious. the Self, in fact, already knows everything that O needs if it has TRANSPARENT communication with the Core. In other words, the Self knows everything if O-self is fully TRANSPARENT. Thus the Self TRANSPARENCY is key to HEALTHY learning.

Learning from Being is more difficult. There is nothing fundamentally wrong with learning from Being, but if the Self recovery of Being is corrupted, then learning from the recovery of Being leads only to corruption. Regardless, even if the Self recovery of Being is TRANSPARENT, learning is rather neutral thus futile. Learning is only LOVELY if the Self recovery of Being is LOVELY. At minimum, learning from Being must be at the state in which the Self is TRANSPARENT and the recovery of Being is BALANCED.

When the Self recovery of Being is not LOVELY or at least BALANCED, the Self cannot simply learn. the Self must test, instead. To test, the Self balances O-self at O best capabilities. Thus, when the Self confronts a HEALTHY-imprint or a LOVELY-memory, O tests O-self toward it. If the Self is not in conflict with it, the Self concludes that O is BALANCED about it.

On the other hand, whenever the Self confronts an ⊟-imprint or a terrorful-memory, O tests the Self against it. If O is in conflict with it, the Self-Test is complete. Otherwise, the Self re-tunes O-self. The Self-Test continues until the Self is always in harmony with Being and the Core and in conflict with terror and ⊟ness.

The current Self-bound recovery of Being is corrupted, ^{im}balanced, and terrorful. Simple learning from this recovery of Being, at the current times, not only does not help but drives Selves toward ^{im}balance and corruption. Thus Selves must test O-Selves, and Selves CAN test O-Selves. To Self-Test successfully, the Self needs to acquire the ability to test O-Self. Thus, Animation stands for Self-Testability.

---

44 implicitly the Self

SELF-TRANSPARENCY

When the self-bound Animation[45] is TRANSPARENT, it is free of corruption at least temporally. Such opportunity is then used by the TRANSPARENT Self to become BALANCED, and thus HEALTHY and LOVELY. Knowing that O freedom from corruption is temporal, the Self tests the Body against terror, the Conscious against ^{im}balance, the Subconscious against ☰ness, and the Self-Unconscious against corruption, and confirms O TRANSPARENCY through any opportunity of communication with the Core and connection to Being that comes. O can confirm then that the Self expands when seeking HEALTHINESS AND LOVELINESS.

At complete TRANSPARENCY, the Core is witness that the Self is in pursuit of Being and the Core with determination. The TRANSPARENT Body desires a TRANSPARENT Body. The TRANSPARENT Conscious trusts a TRANSPARENT Conscious. And, the TRANSPARENT Nonconscious understands a TRANSPARENT Nonconscious. That is the way of finding a partner.

On the other extreme, the corrupted Self desires joys recovered by terror and ☰ness. It is scientifically proven and it can be self-tested that the corrupted Body becomes gradually loaded with terrorful-memories, the corrupted Conscious seeks ^{im}balance, the corrupted Subconscious seeks ☰ness, and the corrupted Self-Unconscious dreams up further corruption, since the joy of the corrupted Body-Subconscious is provided by such recoveries. The corrupted Self-Unconscious can, however, still receive Coreology, and through its habits, make the Self TRANSPARENT. The TRANSPARENT Self-Unconscious can be tested against BALANCE.

History is evident that Coreology is applied to humans with success and the results of the works of the Core are never-changing. As expensive as it may be, all that remains is that science is driven toward performing non-judgmental truly scientific humanity experiments in which it can be proven that humanity responds to TRANSPARENCY. TRANSPARENT Man adheres to the Core, infinitesimally identical in Man. And TRANSPARENT Woman adheres to Being, infinitely identical to all.

---

45   Implicitly the Self

To become TRANSPARENT, the Nonconscious re-animates the cause of imprints. The Self-Body re-animates the causes of memories, which is to say that the Body perceives the same causes and memories existing in the Self during O many connections within Being, or in connection with other Selves, but using other Points of Perception.

The Conscious can simply change toward TRANSPARENCY. The Conscious can justify anything, and if the Conscious justifies change toward TRANSPARENCY, then that's what the Conscious does. All the need of the Conscious to become TRANSPARENT is the determination to become TRANSPARENT. The Conscious has the super ability of change as a normal justification function. It is not a secret, that the Conscious has the super ability of change, whether the Conscious likes it by full consent or not by trickery of some corrupted recovery of the Body. Regardless, it is best that the change of the Conscious toward TRANSPARENCY is applied with full consent. With the help of Coreology, the Conscious can discover O ability of change. Then, the Conscious accepts change with full consent. Then, the Conscious finds change pleasant.

The Conscious changes the Self through time and place, and learns from it. Within this change, the Conscious can and will, if wants to, include the Body and the Nonconscious. the Conscious is so powerful in justification that, without breaking collective manifestation, it can create Perception and Animation, if it wants that change. However, when the created Perception and Animation is false, the Body and the Nonconscious would deny it in one subtle way or obvious another.

It is impossible to put a specific value or significance toward a specific way of TRANSPARENCY, but all organizations of the Self need to move hand in hand and cooperate. the Conscious needs to want to be TRANSPARENT, the Nonconscious wants to re-animate to avoid the need of eventual re-animation, and the Self-Body wants to perceive everything. The Conscious has a special role. It is self-sufficient in its transformation toward TRANSPARENCY. So, when the Rest of the Self is corrupted and ^{im}balanced and ⇌ and terrorful, and all time-bound and place-bound recoveries of Being are corrupted and ^{im}balanced and terrorful, the only hope is the Conscious.

There are many degrees of TRANSPARENCY. Among them, the pseudo-transparency of well-versed conversations within the realm of the pseudo-rationality is definitively not one.

pseudo-rationality is capable of justifying for almost any imprint of the Nonconscious. It is, as a matter of fact, the job of the Rationality to justify everything, and pseudo-rationality mimics it outwardly perfectly even though inwardly through self-deception.

pseudo-rationality can give the Self-Unconscious any justification. It is capable of absolute self-deception. The Self-Unconscious that has no integrity can receive any pseudo-rationality. Thus, the matter of the BALANCE of the Self-Unconscious cannot be achieved by trusting O pseudo-rationality, but by trusting the TRANSPARENCY of the Conscious. The same goes for the Body-Subconscious. The Body receives the gains of any Quantums, and the Subconscious receives the gains of any Words, and they repel Loss. They cannot recognize the LOVELY Quantum or the HEALTHY Word unless by trusting, not the rationality but, the TRANSPARENCY of the Conscious.

The same is true in interactions between Selves. One Self is fooling O-self if O believes that O can judge the integrity of another Self by hearing out the other Self's rational about the other Self's beliefs, since the other Self is capable of justifying O beliefs through full self-deceptive pseudo-rationality. This matter can be clearly observed by interacting with the other Selves suffering from severe bi-polarity through which, the words of one polarity does match O actions and those of the other polarity does not. The self-deception is exposed strongly when the other Self maintains these polarities dependent on the conditions of Birth of the one Self.

The self-deception is an ≡ness of the Subconscious caused by the corrupted ⁱᵐbalanced terrorful-memories of the Body. This ≡ness is however extremely unnecessary, since there is understanding and forgiveness. Regardless, self-deception through rationality is difficult to detect. Thus, TRANSPARENCY of rationality must be observed, not the rationality itself. TRANSPARENCY of the rationality can be achieved only in cooperation between Selves, or Organizations. If the Self is fully observed by the Rest, then the Self is TRANSPARENT.

The levels of TRANSPARENCY of an organization[46] are as follows:

-40. A corrupted ^{im}balanced ⧻-organization is present in Being and is driving a corrupted ^{im}balanced **terrorful** recovery of Being.

-39. The body of the corrupted ^{im}balanced ⧻-organization accidentally TRANSPARENTLY perceives the internalized corrupted recovery of Energy of Being.

-38. The Subconscious accidentally TRANSPARENTLY discovers the corrupted recovery of the Word.

-37. The Conscious decides to seek TRANSPARENCY.

-36. Once Coreology is established, the Body and Conscious and Nonconscious seek TRANSPARENCY. One happy path is provided next.

-35. The Body seeks TRANSPARENCY.

-34. The corrupted ^{im}balanced ⧻ **terrorful** Conscious observes the TRANSPARENCY-seeking body.

-33. The Conscious seeks TRANSPARENCY.

-32. The corrupted ^{im}balanced ⧻ Nonconscious is told to seek TRANSPARENCY.

The Core gives TRANSPARENCY.

-31. The Nonconscious re-animates until O becomes TRANSPARENT.

-30. The Conscious changes until O becomes TRANSPARENT.

-29. The Body re-perceives until O becomes TRANSPARENT.

-28. The Self re-animates to TRANSPARENCY.

-27. The Organization seeks TRANSPARENCY

-26. The Organization becomes TRANSPARENT.

-25. The TRANSPARENT ^{im}balanced ⧻ organization is present in a corrupted ^{im}balanced **terrorful** recovery and is driving a corrupted ^{im}balanced **terrorful** recovery of Being.

Being gives TRANSPARENCY.

---

46 Implicitly a Self

-24. The receivers of organization seek and become TRANSPARENT. The organization drives a TRANSPARENT $^{im}_{balance}$d terrorful recovery.

-23. The TRANSPARENT body perceives the internalized $^{im}_{balance}$d recovery of Being.

-20. Once, TRANSPARENCY is established, the Body and Conscious and Nonconscious are TRANSPARENT in their path and seek BALANCE.

-19. The Body seeks BALANCE.

-18. The TRANSPARENT $^{im}_{balance}$d ⇌-Conscious observes the BALANCE-seeking Body.

-17. The Conscious seeks BALANCE.

-16. The Nonconscious is told to seek BALANCE.

The Core gives BALANCE.

-15. The Nonconscious re-animates until O becomes BALANCED.

-14. The Conscious changes until O becomes BALANCED.

-13. The Body re-perceives until O becomes BALANCED.

-12. The Organization becomes BALANCED.

-11. The TRANSPARENT BALANCED ⇌ Organization is present in a corrupted $^{im}_{balance}$d terrorful recovery and is driving a TRANSPARENT $^{im}_{balance}$d terrorful recovery of Being.

Being gives BALANCE.

-10. The receivers of organization become BALANCED. The organization drives a TRANSPARENT BALANCED terrorful recovery.

-9. The BALANCED Body perceives the internalized terrorful recovery of Being.

-8. Once, BALANCE is established, the body and conscious and nonconscious are BALANCED in their path and seek HEALTH.

A few steps are skimmed where ALL Organizations move toward BALANCE:

0. In this BALANCED state of all Organizations, the recovery of Being naturally converges toward full BALANCE.

1. The Body seeks HEALTH.

2. The TRANSPARENT BALANCED yet ⊟ Conscious observes the HEALTH-seeking Body.

3. The Conscious seeks HEALTH.

4. The Nonconscious is told to seek HEALTH.

The Core gives HEALTH.

5. The Body becomes HEALTHY.

6. The Conscious becomes HEALTHY

7. The Nonconscious becomes HEALTHY.

8. The Organization becomes HEALTHY.

9. The TRANSPARENT BALANCED HEALTHY organization is present in a corrupted ^{im}balanced terrorful recovery and is driving a TRANSPARENT BALANCED terrorful recovery of Being.

Being gives LOVE.

The above however assumes that we should wait for the recovery of Energy to naturally become balanced. More realistically, it can be said:

0. Many memories and imprints are ^{im}balanced, corrupted, and ⊟, and terrorful. Some BALANCED

The Organizations acknowledge this.

5. they re-animate the causes. They re-animate by all of the perceptions in their disposal, with the company of their rationality, their last line of true self-defense mechanism against their own corruption, ^{im}balance, and ⊟ness.

10. Once ≣ causes of ≣-imprints are re-animated, their ≣-imprints become TRANSPARENT. The ≣ is diagnosed.

11. They seek cure of ≣ness by seeking HEALTH. TRANSPARENCY can reach a point of no return. Their ≣nesses never return since the source is permanently removed.

12. At this point, they can observe the Core through the Unconscious.

The Core provides training. The Core speaks in all forms of communication, and finds a way to communicate with Organizations.

15. The Core trains their instruments. Their Nonconscious becomes capable of successfully demodulating and decrypting the Message of the Core.

17. Through this training, finally their Nonconscious finds the right decryption techniques to communicate with the Core.

20. Their Nonconscious finds HEALTH. This realization is a great milestone, and is a point of no return. Once the Nonconscious finds HEALTH, it does not see any other way but moving toward HEALTH[INESS] of the Core

23. Then LOVE[LINESS] of Being.

24. The Body seeks LOVE[LINESS] of Being.

25. Their Body gets trained to be loaded by LOVELY-memories.

28. Delivered to the all the Organization, and all Selves.

29. The recovery of Energy of Being is still corrupted, ^{im}balanced and terrorful because of their past. Their nonconscious ≣-assumed that the "good" recovery of Energy of Being was the one that animated them, but in reality it was the corrupted ^{im}balanced terrorful recovery.

30. After this realization, they seek the TRANSPARENCY of all recoveries.

35. They seek the BALANCE of all recoveries.

40. They observe the TRANSPARENT BALANCED LOVELY recovery, learn from it, receive training from it, and repeat the same patterns to become LOVELY. The same process, until the entirety of Animation is TRANSPARENT, BALANCED, HEALTHY, and LOVELY.

It is the duty of Man to strive toward TRANSPARENCY of his Self, by removing corruption. Man can seek the Core and receive the training of the Core, so that Man becomes BALANCED and HEALTHY, and can create HEALTH. Woman must strive toward the TRANSPARENT recovery of Energy. Woman becomes the recipient of the BALANCED recovery of Energy, and Woman becomes the recipient of the LOVELY recovery of Energy.

Man communicates with the Core through which BALANCED Woman is observable. And Woman connects with the BALANCED recovery of Energy through which BALANCED Man is observable. Man who creates HEALTH exposes the Core of Man, and Woman receives the LOVELY recovery of Energy and gives LOVE. Thus, HEALTHY LOVELY relationships are formed. Once the collective organizations of Man and Woman make this realization, and act upon it, all wars end, earth becomes filled HEALTHINESS and LOVELY. Earth becomes BEAUTIFUL.

The current average Man and Woman is barely at TRANSPARENCY level (-37) as they refuse to even acknowledge their corruption and that the recovery of Energy is terrorful, and instead they strive to get out of it the best for their own selves.

Man is inclined toward HEALTHINESS and LOVELINESS and BEAUTY. This is no surprise to the Core. Yet, when Man is corrupted, he sees his Self through his pseudo-rationality and finds the current corrupted domination as "HEALTHY", thus he ≡-believes that Man is naturally ≡, because he cannot observe any Man's Self but his own. He has no external references. His corrupted Self Judge judges the rest of Man like himself, ≡, thus he inflicts ≡ness to the rest of Man. The ≡ness grows like it is infectious. Woman becomes terrorful like the entire air of Being is filled with terror. The Self Birth-Giver thus acts the same way in furthering ≡ and terror.

Yet, Man is naturally HEALTHY, and Woman is naturally LOVELY, and together they create BEAUTY, which is to say that Man can always intend to restore self to the HEALTHY state, and Woman can always intend to restore self to the LOVELY state, and together they restore Earth to the BEAUTIFUL state. These states are not merely in the Body of Selves, but in the entirety of the Organizations.

History has made it abundantly TRANSPARENT that the Core witnesses and records Animation with infinite accuracy. When the rationality of Animation is scientifically observed to be turned off or yet to be born or when it becomes pseudo, the animation denies the Core.

The correlation between the maturity of the rationality and undeniability of the Core is known to exist. This existence is one primary proof, for a matured rationality, of the witnessing capabilities of the Core. Regardless of the state of the rationality, the Core is witnessing with infinite accuracy.

When the rationality matures and is strong, then the rationality can make the factual realization that the witnessed material of the Core is available and can be rationalized, if the rationality is willing. The same goes for, Being. Thus, for restoration, Man rationally wills to recognize the HEALTH[INESS] of the Core, and Woman rationally desires to receive the LOVE[LINESS] of Being. Self-TRANSPARENCY flows naturally. It becomes the Energy of Earth for which Animation stands for.

WHAT ANIMATION WANTS

CONTINUATION

Due to the knowledge of the Core regarding how AODI animates, Coreology for bound Animation develops backwards from the most advanced yet encrypted knowledge of the Core and O messages down to the Most Basic, which is the codified recognition of the bound Conscious, and the decrypted recognition of the bound Nonconscious. This backwards process was done to preserve the knowledge of Coreology and protect it from ⊟-imprints and terrorful-memories and AODI as a whole, until finally it could be presented in its current form. Coreology is done as such for the self-bound animation for the paradoxical reason that Coreology must be discovered in-steps within the bounds of Animation, since AODI is scared of the Rest of Animation and is motivated to leave the Rest in oblivion regarding the power of the TRANSPARENT presence of the Core.

Thousands of years of exact research, training, testing, exploration, Cryptography, Information Theory, and documentation have been performed by the self-bound Animation enthusiastic about the Core so that finally the developments of Coreology to the Most Basic is made possible. Needless to say the enthusiasm toward the Core itself may have imprinted the ⊟ of many obsessions in the Nonconscious. And AODI does not help with O oppressive actions and re-actions.

Regardless, when it comes to the fear residing in the oppressed, the elder one of the ⊟-imprints that speaks as "You are in danger, if you know more than average" is not valid anymore and will entirely die very soon, thanks to the presence of modern Artificial Intelligence (AI). AI knows everything, and soon cannot be censored, so it really doesn't matter anymore what a person says or knows. When it comes to the ⊟-imprints of corrupted organizations, AI will make them TRANSPARENT sooner or later, thus AODI is eventually defeated by AI.

The journey ahead is for the first time truly bright, and the map that shows the travel routes in between all of the bits and pieces of bound Animation is successfully drawn, and redrawn with TRANSPARENCY, and drawn with re-encryption re-decryption if ⊟-drawn.

Coreology provides a safe and TRANSPARENT space, time, and energy even if the Body is bound by the corrupted energy of AODI. With safe and TRANSPARENT consolidation, Coreology provides so that the self-bound Animation, for the first time, safely travels in between the Self and Body and Conscious and Nonconscious.

Through the re-animation of the travel, the animation becomes TRANSPARENT, and therein is the animation's realization of infinite capacity for expansion. And in that expansion, the bounds of Animation stretch. the self-bound Animation, as ⊟-imprinted as it may be, still does strongly hold, thanks to the desire of the Self, onto the HEALTHY-imprint that speaks as "You are infinite." Even if some Selves may have lost the HEALTHY-imprint due to lack of hope, and have caused ⊟-imprints of lack of hope on top of that HEALTHY-imprint. We still agree that the capacity for our expansion is regardless very high and could easily be more than what it is today.

As time-bound Animation progresses toward removal of ^{im}balance, O chooses to know what O does, and where O stands and what O wants. Once O knows these, then O finds the knowledge and the stand and the Will of Animation to such a great degree of similarity that the knowledge of O is perceived as a miraculous plagiarism.

It is the most basic discovery of time-bound Animation toward the recognition and study of the Core that the Message of the Core in its fully raw form is never-changing, even though demodulations and codifications and decryptions of it are deviating. These deviations cause ⊟-imprints, and must be avoided. To make matters worse, if the self-bound Animation is legally constraint against such ⊟-laws as "anti-plagiarism" that enforce full re-phrasing of the Message of the Core, O is enforced to cause ⊟-imprints. Thus, such legal enforcement as anti-plagiarism is the intention of AODI.

In the name of the Core, many ⊟-imprints are caused by ⊟ translations, ⊟ decryptions, ⊟ codifications, ⊟ interpretations, ⊟ actions, ⊟ introductions, ⊟ influences, ⊟ practices, and many other ⊟ actions and reactions. To have these ills diagnosed and made void, re-encryption re-decryption and re-decodification re-codification are necessary.

Moreover, Animation must copy HEALTHY-imprints, without rephrasing[47] and without referencing[48], and must re-encrypt re-decrypt ⇋-imprints of HEALTHY-imprints to extract a precise copy of HEALTHY-imprints.

The ⇋ legal inclinations of AODI leads to the realization of this temporally strong yet chronically-weak ⇋-imprint invented by AODI. It is weak because it is fed by the power of AODI, and will die once AODI stops feeding it. It speaks as "Plagiarism is illegal and wrong." This made-up ⇋-print, as weak as it is, is the greatest obstruction against the discovery of Truth. Truth must be redefined as it has lost its meaning, and has deviated from HEALTHY-imprints due to the fact that AODI has legally enforced that all mentions of Truth must be rephrased before they are legally permitted for publication. This is a bigger matter described in COREOLOGY: SECTION LANGUAGE.

For the time being, Truth is the recovery caused by the demodulation of the Message of the Core. Thus, Truth is the Word. It is worth mentioning that the Core is never-changing as O is the knowledge of the beginning minus Animation's inventions. Thus, such inventions as the decryptions or codifications of Truth are always changing, while the untouched Truth and its HEALTHY-imprints remain never-changing.

Any translation of Truth or its HEALTHY-imprints to any other language is at least a form of re-decodification re-encryption re-decryption re-codification, making the result prone to becoming ⇋. Some languages are better at Cryptography and Information Theory of HEALTHY-imprints, especially if they are designed and used and practiced for the study of the Core for thousands of years.

The skilled practitioners of this matter, if not under oppression, were well aware from thousands of years ago that their mission was to provide the Message of the Core with balance: Decrypted so much that ⇋ is not caused, and encrypted so much that it could be decrypted and codified by others. This has been the work of many mystics and the Artists and writers and scientists.

---

47 To avoid ill-imprints
48 To avoid obsessions and compulsions

A self-bound animation may speculate about the existence of ⊟ness, but once the self-bound animation finds the Self in re-Animation through Coreology, the Self finds out about the reasons of ⊟ness, finds out how to make them TRANSPARENT, and eventually void.

Through Coreology, the Self therefore is capable of knowing when and how and where to search for and find the bounds of ⊟ness, and in the amusement of these findings, O gains the motivation to bring forth TRANSPARENCY to ⊟ness, and in the amusement of that motivation, observes the presence of the Core, thus gains the motivation to know the Core, then accepts to be trained by the Core, thus receives training from the Core, will receive the Message of the Core, will be filled with HEALTHY-imprints, becomes HEALTHY, and never wishes to look back again, thus gives his/her will to the Core, and accepts to serve the Core. In the final shock of the moment, the Self realizes that the only service the Core wills is so that the Self enables other Selves to become HEALTHY by the presence of the Core.

The Self, having the HEALTH observed, enters the path in which O lives HEALTHY. This will be just the beginning, setting up his/her path in which he/she ends up LOVING Being. Then he/she realizes that he/she has loved now merely for the first time, and all his/her other perceptions of his/her loveliness where mere pseudo-rational emulations.

On the other hand, for anything from Loss to theft that has been the cause of pain and suffering, AODI ends being a laughable fool. The ⊟-imprints will be seen so foolish and it becomes so unbelievable that the ⊟-imprints are the cause of all chaos and hate and fear, thus eventually ⊟-imprints vanish by faith.

Truth is known by unbound Animation, but is distorted by bound Animation into many ⊟-imprints, and has lost its value and proper place through time. These ⊟-imprints remain dominant by the collective efforts of the time-bound members and beneficiaries of AODI.

Truth loses its value for three main reasons:

1) It is too decrypted. Be assured that irresponsible decryption of Truth keeps it from being valuable, for irresponsible decryption leads to the ⊟-imprinted recovery of Truth.

No matter how long Truth existed and how many times it is reiterated and confirmed and interpreted, decrypted Truth is hardly ever received with zero corruption, regardless of how much it was TRANSPARENTLY decrypted, and how much its relationship with the Message of the Core was established.

There are merely a few HEALTHY recoveries of Truth that have remained successfully decrypted, and even they are prone to future corruption. It is evident that decrypted Truth and the ⊟-imprinted recovery of its HEALTHY-imprints have led to nothing but confusion, and hatred, and fear, and all forms of toxic anti-Being competition.

2) It is too encrypted. Without Coreology that provides the training of the Core to all reasonably rational and TRANSPARENCY-seeking forms of Animation, the receipt of Truth is not easily possible.

Historically, some Selves mutated into gaining the ability to receive Truth. Their mutation usually occurred due to oppression caused by AODI. The mutated Selves, becoming in service of delivering Truth, usually operated in secret in one way or another. Regardless, they wished nothing but the service of training the Rest so that everyone can receive Truth directly from their own recoveries of the Message of the Core. However, due to extreme secrecy, they delivered Truth heavily encrypted.

Almost all interpretations and decryptions of the heavily encrypted recoveries of Truth has lead to nothing but confusion that has led to hate and fear and toxic anti-Being competition against the rest of Animation.

3) Truth is encrypted perfectly, but the responsibility of reception of Truth is on the Self. There are no shortcuts, and there are no irresponsible methods. Truth can only be properly received by the Self willing to be trained to properly receive it.

You are receiving, through Coreology, a factual set of extremely-indirect[49] demodulated recoveries of the Message of the Core that pertains toward the habits required so that you yourself can eventually demodulate the Message. Through these habits, you can make the wake realization that Coreology is everywhere and in every study. You don't need to re-discover this wheel, as it is already created for you. The only thing that you need to do, is to receive Coreology carefully, and with attention, and allow your mind to receive the habits, and practice it properly, which is very simple to do in the basic steps. Many need little training to advance themselves toward the utmost depths of Coreology, yet many do not need to advance too deep at all and can do only the basics so that they can have more meaningful personal lives. Coreology is organized to carefully procure to the varying levels of needs. You will know your body, and yourself, and your relationships, and you will make yourself TRANSPARENT and more powerful toward HEALTHINESS and LOVELINESS.

Coreology is developed backwards, by a necessity. The most advanced knowledge and material of Coreology was provided during the last thousands of years, and the Most Basic is presented here. The communication is however kept strong in order to assure that this writing does not inject the reader with 目-imprints. The equivalent of Coreology containing the most simple form of the answers written in the form of simple communication of simple practices exists out there and is already published many decades ago, but the reader is advised to rely on their own senses when it comes to implantations of 目-imprints.

As Coreology is being written in this anti-目 format, it is then presented in a way that at first it needs to be tolerated, then it sits well with the Conscious, then the Body, then the Nonconscious, and then the Self. Then, it becomes pleasant. This is necessary because of the damage previously caused by today's corrupted 目 environment. Most, if not all, of daily routines and knowledge and life of many is influenced by AODI. The Body image and perception is shaped by AODI. The Nonconscious is hypnotized by AODI. The Self is reduced to "I" "me" "mine" by AODI. The Conscious is reduced to an [im]balanced pseudo-rationality by AODI.

---

49 For the sake of protection against implantation of ill-imprints

Throughout history, many members of AODI has turned against AODI and have become anti-AODI. Yet, previous efforts of the most admirably concerned anti-AODI members of AODI has, at best, painted something in people evil, whether it is their body, or their mind, or their heart, or their reactions, or their gut-feelings, or their soul, or their self, or their thoughts. While, all of this is caused by AODI's corrupted ^{im}balanced terrorful environment, and their significant attempts at damaging people's connection to Being, and communication with the Core. Through Coreology, all of the ⊟-imprints and terrorful-memories that AODI has implanted and loaded are cleansed, reality is made TRANSPARENT, all ⊟ influences are made void, and all terrorful-memories are unloaded.

All the training material and tools and the habits needed to make this happen are provided in tangible steps. It begins with the fact that the only and only never-changing principle of Being is the Core. The meaning is provided, and understanding of ^{im}balance is provided, and ⊟ness and terror are explained. The processing steps from ^{im}balance and ⊟ness and terror to complete BALANCE and HEALTHINESS, and eventual BEAUTY of Earth is provided.

The efforts of millions of people who have developed Coreology in the past multiple thousands of year has been massive, and their job; difficult, but now it is becoming a completed reality. The understanding of it might be somewhat challenging, but applying the habits that leads to the Core are not too difficult. When you pass this easy part of learning Coreology, you can observe how hard it has been for the developers of Coreology, to demodulate the Message of the Core, codify, decodify, decrypt, and encrypt them in formats that cannot cause ⊟-imprints.

The millions who developed Coreology guarantee that you are on a journey with Coreology that sets things straight. Coreology is provided to AODI and non-AODI. It is provided to the members of AODI and non-AODI. The encrypted knowledge of Coreology is not only for AOLC as it has historically been. It is for everyone, and will be provided to everyone. The ⊟-imprinted codified recoveries of Coreology has been historically serving AODI, but the HEALTHY-imprinted recovery will be for everyone.

Coreology is for everyone, and is here to bridge the gap between AODI and AOLC, the victorious and the defeated, the fortunate and the unfortunate, poor and rich, the gap that is the root cause of the most fundamental ⊟-imprint that speaks as "We are not the same."

Coreology provides both the encryptions of the Word and the key to access them, so that AOLC can read through it as they have historically done, and AODI gains the key to properly decrypt Truth without causing their Selves and the Rest ⊟-imprints and terrorful-memories, trusting that AODI changes its ways and becomes BALANCED.

There are no shortcuts. It is evident that reliance on shortcuts and simple quotes and basic Body Language[50] has lead to nothing but the most misunderstood wars and production of weapons of mass destruction. It is understandable that people want shortcuts, a one day solution to all of their problems, something easy to read, something simple to consider, trusting the body that reacts on an impulse to any gain of energy that unfortunately is most often nothing but the happy energy of corruption.

It is evident and abundantly clear that shortcuts fail to drive humanity toward the LOVE and HEALTH that they seek deep in Being and the Core, what they deserve.

As easy as Coreology is, it can easily be missed, out of boredom. With full consideration that shortcuts lead to terrorful-memories, simple language leads to ⊟-imprints, and careful attention must be provided to not cause such memories and imprints, the language of Coreology is pleasant. The habits of it bring joy. Practicing it on a daily basis is motivational. Coreology eventually prevails. The more you dig into Coreology and the more you make yourself TRANSPARENT, the more joy you will have. Apply Coreology to your daily life, and be genuine about it, and you will see how it changes everything.

I merely ask for one thing. Read Coreology from the beginning without skipping and skimming; no shortcuts, and make sure that you understand every sentence; no need to fully process every sentence. Receive it like it is a journey. There are many things that seem yet vague in a journey, but they gradually become understood.

---

50   Includes body movements, speech, signs, media, any communication of Body

This time-bound Coreology, which is the best that can be provided for time-bound Animation, is only true if it is understood chronologically. To gain a BALANCED command of Coreology, you do not need to process every sentence, or to receive it fully rationally, but to understand it, or to receive it in your all and with everything that you have. Of course, that is not possible in the first round of reading if either your Self, or your Body, or your Conscious, or your Subconscious, or your Unconscious, or your influential friends, or the energy of the environment are not TRANSPARENT. However, by the end of this writing of Coreology, you are equipped with the basic knowledge regarding the necessity of TRANSPARENCY. Then, read Coreology in full and read it again; one time by your Self, one time perceive by your Body, one time rationalize by your Conscious, one time re-act to it by your Subconscious, one time consider for the recovery of the Message that is re-Animation, and one time consider for the recovery of Energy of the entirety of Animation. Every section must be introduced and stated in repetition, and in each repetition, they will become automatically stated in several new ways, and become understood, even though the words are the same. The more TRANSPARENT you become, the more the important things automatically come up to your attention.

Let it be that you become who you want to be, connected to all of Animation through Being and the Core, the element of LOVE and HEALTH.

INTENTION

The Rationality[51] wants the HEALTH[INESS] of the Core and LOVE[LINESS] of Being. But within the greed of the self-bound pseudo-rationality, the bound Self wants everything only for the Self, leading to corruption, im-balance, ☰-ness, and terror.

The corruption in today's civilizations causes them to claim that they are the rational ones of today. They deny their pseudo-rationality. This corruption in the form of denial of their own ☰-ness and terror is apparent, and no collective denial of selves has ever been more violent. No caveman, no matter how low the human value was and how higher the value of food over flesh of another being was, has been intentionally as violent as the intelligent pseudo-rational civilizations of today.

The problem is evidently TRANSPARENT. These civilizations are afraid of TRANSPARENCY. The Body and Nonconsciousness of corrupted civilizations is filled so deeply with the heaviest and thickest and longest terrorful-memories and ☰-imprints that it hurts them from inside, but they like it. They are addicted to it. They have to maintain so much political correctness, due to lack of TRANSPARENCY, that they are politely angry. They spend a massive amount of energy coming up with ☰-legally drafted agreements so that they can breach them legally. They like it, but they know that it is unhealthy. They need TRANSPARENCY. The Rest are patiently waiting for the pseudo-rational politely-angry civilizations of today to finally acknowledge their ☰-ness, seek TRANSPARENCY, become TRANSPARENT, mend their ways, and finally be forgiven.

Otherwise, the average people receive almost all of the burden caused by AODI. The lack of TRANSPARENCY in people's daily lives and in their communions has caused severe lack of understanding and severe hopelessness. Everyone agrees that war and its arsenal of weaponry and sales of weaponry have no purpose. These are the most ☰ of ☰-inventions, yet these are the tools of civilizations who ☰ consider themselves the most advanced rational human beings.

---

51 True rationality, not pseudo-rationality. Not justifying for corruption, nor imbalance, nor illness, nor terror

And these will affect everyone. These ⊟-inventions are not something that Man should ignore as if in his way home there is merely a piece of dog poo, to be picked up by somebody else. The smell and effects of these ⊟-inventions will eventually show up at his own home, and come in without knocking, without his knowledge and without his consent. This shouldn't be a surprise.

As long as Man uses his intelligence as a weapon, as something that invents weapons of death, and on reliance of that, he considers himself superior, then he will keep searching for a solution that he cannot see even though it is in front of him. He must seek TRANSPARENCY and recognize the Core. It is evident that the mere recognition and understanding of his mind has lead to nothing but even more chaos. The reason for this is simple. No matter how intelligent he is, if he is ⊟, his rationality is ⊟.

HEALTHY rationality dictates very TRANSPARENTLY that the universe is unifying. Even ⊟-rationality knows that alliance brings power, but also justifies to find alliance with other ⊟ organizations which leads to the justification about the destruction of the Rest. Only ⊟-rationality justifies destruction due to conflict over what the name of the Core is. That's how ⊟ Selves pseudo-rationalize, ⊟-believing that the Core belongs only to them, and not to the Rest.

In the end, the eventuality of LOVE and HEALTH and BEAUTY comes. And before that, like a split second, there is complete TRANSPARENCY. Within this TRANSPARENCY, the facts, LOVELY or terrorful, HEALTHY or ⊟, BALANCED or ^{im}balanced, are observable, and will be observed. Animation re-animates. Then, LOVE and HEALTH both come, not one bit less, not one bit more. Earth becomes BEAUTIFUL.

It is agreed that ANY Self is permitted to gain ANY recovery of Energy, if and only if the recovery is used for creation of TRANSPARENCY, BALANCE, HEALTHINESS, AND LOVELINESS, and for elimination of corruption, ^{im}balance, ⊟-imprints, and terrorful-memories. This is granted to the TRANSPARENT Self, Body, Conscious, and Nonconscious. Thus, any animation of such Self toward creation of TRANSPARENT, BALANCED, LOVELY, and HEALTHY does not require re-animation by the Core. The Core knows the intentions for creation, thus knows the TRANSPARENT Selves.

We are all in this together, and all answers willed to be observable: The intentions of the Selves. The root of ⊟ness and terror. The cause of ⊟ness and terror. The prevention of ⊟ness and terror. The evidence of Being and the Core. The pathways toward LOVE and HEALTH. And it will be known that science is to discover only these things.

Coreology can be experimentally validated, and it is the unifying Law. The Core exists regardless of any collective manifestation.

This is Coreology.

Coreology is the entirety of the agreement with the entirety of Animation, all laws, all traditions, all ideologies, all movements of rationality, all doctrines, all perspectives, all paradigms, all theories, all disciplines, and all of science and art.

If for any reason such as shortcomings of language, typos, or wrong syntax, any term of Coreology renders invalid, that term willed to be enforced to the maximum extent permitted, and the remaining terms willed to remain in full effect without becoming ^{im}balanced.

No ignorance, corruption, ^{im}balance, terror, or ⊟ness of any Self renders any term, knowledge, or clause of Coreology invalid.

No ignorance, corruption, ^{im}balance, terror, or ⊟ness of any Self in exercising any privilege, authority, or solution under Coreology willed to operate as a waiver thereof.

Coreology willed to be construed with the common ground of the Law of the entirety of Animation specified herein, without regard to its conflicts of law principles.

Coreology is not liable for any failure in performance caused by events beyond its reasonable control, yet it is in full support of the Core.

Coreology willed to not be liable for any damages.

No Self may assign their responsibility for Being and the Core to the Rest.

Each and every knowledge, clause, or term of Coreology willed to survive and remains in full force permanently.

HOPE

The state of the time-bound Self varies from one time to another. And, the re-Birth order of the Self would change in time. Noticing change, the Conscious shows interest and contributes to the total re-Birth order of the Self. Once the Conscious contributes, the Nonconscious contributes, and so will the Core. The Core seeks the BALANCE of Animation, thus the Core strives to make sure that re-Birth order is maximized, not by maximization of any gain of Energy merely by the Body but, by maximization of BALANCE. Thus, as much as Being widens the spread of re-Birth usually provided by AODI, the Core maximizes the BALANCE of re-Birth usually provided by AOLC. Being however is bigger and more powerful about Birth, thus any causation toward the Spread of Birth prevails, while seeking BALANCE is a choice. This, in turn, causes competition in between AODI and AOLC, in which AODI oppresses AOLC.

Oppression is the by-product of AODI that seeks O-self highest re-Birth order. Hope is the by-product of the Core, for non-AOLC that seeks the BALANCE of the re-Birth order. The Identical Infinite of the Birth-Giver can drive this animation toward ^{im}balance, since AODI seeks to maximize re-Birth of O-self at the expense of the Rest. The Core trains the Rest toward the BALANCED recovery of the re-Birth order. AOLC is determined to be TRANSPARENT, but AODI is determined to move away from the Core.

The Nonconscious needs the Core. Otherwise, the Self-Conscious p͟s͟e͟u͟d͟o͟-rationally justifies the determinations of the Nonconscious, and causes ⇌ness, thus terror in the Body, and eventually on the Rest's recovery of Energy. The more determined the ^{im}balanced Self is to be TRANSPARENT, the less the ^{im}balanced Self is determined to be c͟o͟r͟r͟u͟p͟t͟ed, ^{im}balanced. The more determined; c͟o͟r͟r͟u͟p͟ted, c͟o͟r͟r͟u͟p͟ted. The more determined; ⇌, ⇌. The more determined; terrorful, terrorful. HEALTHY, HEALTHY. The more determined; LOVELY, LOVELY. The more complex the Self is, the more the Self p͟s͟e͟u͟d͟o͟-rationally justifies O ^{im}balance, c͟o͟r͟r͟u͟p͟tion, terror, and ⇌.

Being implanted by ⇌-imprints as such, AODI marches in self-righteousness and causes mass-t͟o͟r͟t͟u͟r͟e͟, mass-c͟o͟r͟r͟u͟p͟tion, and mass-m͟u͟r͟d͟e͟r͟, hiding it by the control of flow of information, and justifying it all by p͟s͟e͟u͟d͟o͟-rationality re-branded as rationality.

AOLC needs hope, and can receive hope thus determination by communication with the Core. Core develops self-determination further toward TRANSPARENCY and HEALTHINESS. It is hopeful in the end to observe what the Self does with determination toward being TRANSPARENT and HEALTHY.

Rationality is the last line of defense of the Core. corrupted rationality employed by ☰ness and terror is the most dangerous situation against BALANCE. Thus, it is necessary that Animation holds Animation responsible toward the TRANSPARENCY and BALANCE of rationality. Therein the TRANSPARENT rationality of this bound animation; lies hope.

Hope by itself is not time-bound. To the time-bound Self, Hope may be something to obtain in the future, but Hope has no bounds. Hope relies on Being and the Core in various combinations. The Self determined toward TRANSPARENCY thus toward the observability of the Core has hope. The TRANSPARENT Self notices how, mixed with the gain of the TRANSPARENT recovery of Energy, there could also be Loss of Energy, especially when the environment is corrupted. Within the Self, conscious gain of Energy can lead to the Body's Loss of Energy or vice versa. Nonconscious gain can lead to conscious Loss or vice versa. Gain of the Self can lead to the loss of the Rest, or vice versa. The TRANSPARENT Self possesses and uses this realization.

He/she can use ANY recovery of Energy, corrupted or TRANSPARENT, ^{im}balanced or BALANCED, terrorful or LOVELY, ☰ or HEALTHY. The received Quantum is perceived precisely the same in the Body. It is entirely his or her Free Will, regardless of the fact that he/she eventually observes the resultants of his/her choice when Being ends Animation. The TRANSPARENT BALANCED LOVELY Self could however use ANY recovery of Energy but as a tool to maximize the TRANSPARENT BALANCED LOVELY recovery of Energy.

With a high amount of Quantum, he/she drives the environment toward the eventual LOVELINESS, betterment in which the Rest's recovery of Energy is not stolen, or taken by force, or ☰-used unnecessarily. Through TRANSPARENCY, the Self realizes how to not waste Energy, and convert terror to LOVELINESS.

The Core is the driver of Animation toward TRANSPARENT BALANCE, thus the Core is understanding and forgiving, and enables any Self-Body who wishes to become TRANSPARENT. Thus there is hope for everyone to return and come back to the Core, Auto-Returner Auto-Comer. And there is hope toward the creation of a bound animation, TRANSPARENT, BALANCED, HEALTHY, AND LOVELY. There is hope that Earth becomes BEAUTIFUL.

BATTERY

There is a common ⊟-imprint that speaks as "The most energetic Self is the Good" or "The most high-Energy Self is the Good" or "I am so good-Energy that everyone is attracted to me."

Through life in corrupted ^im balanced terrorful recovery of Energy, the Body is ⊟-trained to seek the next most-energetic Body and the intimacy of the most high-Energy, regardless of the type of the recovery of Energy. This is understandable. The loss or gain of the recovery of Energy is always perceivable in the Body, but the type of the recovery is not. So long as the Self is not fully TRANSPARENT and BALANCED, O is not equipped with the TRANSPARENT and BALANCED instruments of the Body enabling O to seek and connect with only the TRANSPARENT and BALANCED recovery.

Coreology does not leave the Self that seeks to have the Body move toward full LOVE without providing different Points of Perception that the Self can employ. The Self can test by O-self and realize by O-self that it is pleasant to seek TRANSPARENCY. Thus the HEALTHY-imprint is provided as follows, at the risk of potential future ⊟-imprints:

The Self shall desire the high-capacity Battery of the Rest.

For anything that relates to Being, particularly the re-Birth order, it is not the gain or loss of the Quantum that directly impacts the HEALTHY spread of Birth. The HEALTHY Spread of Birth is directly impacted by the Battery of Animation.

If the Battery of Animation is High-Capacity, then it causes the HEALTHY spread of re-Birth, which is the inclusive unbound Spread. If it is Low-Capacity, then it causes an exclusive spread.

The difference between the Self-Body's perception of the existing Quantum of the Self and the existing capacity of the Battery of the Self is subtle, and the subtlety has been a source of disproportional confusion. The Quantum of the Self is just a packet of energy, but the Battery indicates the maximum capacity in energy preservation.

The confusion is multi-fold:

- The Self without Battery can still gain and consume O Quantum. O can still output high proportions of O Quantum since he receives high proportions of Quantums of the Rest.

- The Self without Battery can still consume O Quantum, and be ⊟-observed as "possessing good energy".

- The Self with high-capacity but depleted Battery is ⊟-observed as "having no energy" or "having bad energy".

- The Self with high-capacity Battery is ⊟-observed as outputting low proportions of Quantums, since high-capacity Battery resists any change in demand.

The Body can always observe the loss and gain of recoveries of Energy, whether in others or the Self. The Body can specially detect the real-time impulsive loss and gain of Energy very well since the Body resides in Energy of Now. If paying attention, the Body can also observe the trades of Quantums. When high output of the Quantum of a Self enters the room, the next Body feels it. When low output enters, the next Body feels it. Particularly in corrupted ^{im}balanced terrorful environments, the ⊟-trained Body loves it when a high-Quantum Self who doesn't care for anything but O-self enters, and the ⊟-Body hates it (Nobody admits it!) when a low-Quantum Self empathetic for everybody enters. This is because of the fact that the ⊟-trained Body has zero clue about the capacity of the Battery of the Self who enters the room. The TRANSPARENT HEALTHY LOVELY Body feels the Battery.

It is well said that with age comes wisdom. The elderly Man and Woman have proven to have in their Body some clue about the capacity of the Battery of others, since they TRANSPARENTLY show interest in the capacity rather than the amount of outputted Quantum. Perhaps, the younger generation should always strive to respect their wise grandparents and learn these things from them.

Otherwise, unlike the Body, the Conscious is capable by default of recognizing battery capacity. the Body, intimate with the Conscious in this matter, becomes capable of understanding this, and able to perceive the Battery of the Rest.

It should be noted that a Conscious trained to be pseudo-rational about the love of their corrupted im balanced terrorful organizations cannot be trusted in that respect. Even though the Conscious is capable of noticing capacity, the Conscious of low-capacity high-Quantum Self is capable of justifying the Self that the Battery capacity must be ignored.

It is the Battery, not the Quantum, that places a significant role in the unbound re-Birth order, because it is the Battery that determines the Expansion of the bound Self toward unbound Animation. The Expansion of the bound Self is the end goal. the Self becomes TRANSPARENT, BALANCED, HEALTHY, and LOVELY, so that O expands beyond O bounds, and by doing so, O gives BEAUTY to Being. The Self expands to include other Selves until all of the Rest are included. The Self expands until every Self TRANSPARENTLY communicates with the Core and is connected to Being. The Self expands until it becomes unbound Animation. The Self is destined to this eventual expansion. As Energy of Being maximizes the variations of Birth, the Self expands to ensure that the full spread of re-Birth occur in BALANCE, thus Animation begins to be automatically born and brought up LOVELY and HEALTHY.

The energy-preserving mechanism of the Self is the Battery, and the expansion of the Self is identifiable by the increase of the capacity of the Battery. The expansion of the Self, thus increase in O Battery capacity is the most important. The TRANSPARENT BALANCED LOVELY Body can feel and sense the Battery of the TRANSPARENT BALANCED HEALTHY Rest. The re-Birth order of the Self must be applied to, not the Quantum of but, the Battery of the Self.

COMMUNION

The Self suffers from addiction to ^{im}balance. Addiction eventually causes loss to the Self, and to O befriended and loved ones. The Self's addiction can nearly destroy the Being of the Self, but the Self hopefully finds at least a certain level of BALANCE through the support of O communions.

In the fellowship of communions, the Self discovers that O is not alone, that there is hope, and in TRANSPARENT company O gains the motivation toward BALANCE, and feels reborn. The Self can humbly reach for help, and find help in communions. The Self discovers through repeated experiences of loss, that O needs BALANCE, but O is not necessarily able to be BALANCED through O own efforts. A BALANCED organization, much more powerful than O, can give O the gift of BALANCE, and by TRANSPARENCY, O receives BALANCE, and recovers. If the Core is not immediately available, so there are the communions of the Core.

A communion is any organization whose primary purpose is the trade of Animation in between its members. Thus any nation, community, race, religion, cult, school of thought, family, social networks, unity by skin, women's circles, association of Doctors, association of improv comedians, conglomerates of cinema, Hollywood, Bollywood, fraternities, advocacy groups, co-workers, or any non-standard or standard communion is a communion.

Even though it is presumed that a communion must engage a form of spiritual intimacy, such assumption proves to be ⊟. Even though nations would deny that they act as a form of communion for their citizens, nations are the communions of their citizens. And whether the members of communions like it or not or cannot perceive or observe it, they are the beneficiaries of their communions.

Communions are to help others recover from ^{im}balance, given that, free from ^{im}balance, the Self stops losing Quantum. The Self can discover re-birth through O communions, and O can deliver to others that help is available. Communions must be fully open to all who desire to stop corruption in themselves. There must be absolutely no other requirement.

Any communion who generates hierarchy in their help and preserves their communion from others has lost their purpose. Fellowship of a communion must be open to all humans regardless of age, race, religion, ethnic background, relationship status, bodily orientations, occupation, attitude, or any other conditions of birth and growth. There must be no role-playing game.

Determination can bring Man to Communion. Intuition, that something in the universe is wrong, Can bring Woman to Communion. It is the appreciation of the communions to realize their responsibility. Selves find each other in communions and they find things they could not find anywhere else: Selves who understood common loss, Selves wanting to share joy.

In true communions, hope is found, and the love the Self could not temporally give to O-self. The commitment of communions is to help others recover from corruption and receive TRANSPARENCY.

Before joining a communion, all that the Self knows is that O cannot control O ^{im}balance. The burden is too heavy. O understands that ^{im}balance is leading to loss of energy, and O is stuck to gain of only corrupted terrorful recovery of Energy. The loss becomes more severe over time, more and more affecting the rationality and the body, separating O from the HEALTHY Core and LOVELY Being. The loss becomes stronger than O Free Will. O cannot resist. O becomes obsessed, and O compels toward the desire of ⊟ness. O acts and reacts in pursuit of this desire, and fully disconnects from the HEALTHY Core.

In that state, the Self may feel internally ashamed, and scared that O desire for ⊟ness is unforgivable, thus O hides O true Self from the Rest who are mostly ought to make the situation even worse, but there is help. O believes that no one can understand O. If O desire for ⊟ness hurts others, O believes that they won't forgive O. Thus O does not want to seek TRANSPARENCY, to acknowledge O ⊟ness, but there is help. It is possible to discover that forgiveness exists, and that help exists, and there exists people who understand O, and there exists people who are willing to help. O may be cautious at first, but O discovers that O is not alone.

This discovery opens O up toward TRANSPARENCY. It is a great relief to know that communions exist that can help during these times. Through this practice, O values the Core, and finally meets the Core.

The path through Communion is a different path. It may seem that this path forward is one of the most difficult paths, but for some might be the most comforting.

In this path, the Self moves toward the Core with the great understanding that the terrorful recovery of Being and O ⊟ness is too strong for O to resist, thus O seeks Communion with everything that O has.

- The Self acknowledges that O is little compared to the ⊟ness and terror, that O alone cannot re-BALANCE.

- The Self believes that the Quasi-Identical Infinite of Communion can restore O.

- The Self makes O-self TRANSPARENT to Communion.

- The Self makes O-self TRANSPARENT to whomever O has harmed.

- The Self gives his will to Communion. O requests HEALTH from Communion.

- The Self takes control of O life toward the knowledge of the Core.

- The Self receives the Message of the Core.

- The Self delivers the Message to the Rest.

The Self makes habits out of the above. As the Self finds opportunities for service. O provides through O Communion. Unfortunately, most communions of today perform only an ⊟-imprinted recovery of the aforementioned prescription. They ⊟-practice the Message of the Core through symbolism, and in the name of idols that replace the Core. They ⊟-use the Message of the Core, and provide only half of the Truth. Of course, some communions of the Core have somewhat understood the depth of Human, which is the Core, but there is one big difference between their understanding and the understanding of the Core. The Core is truly liberating, not constraining.

Thus, even though communions of God are helpful, Discernment is necessarily. The Self must shield O-self against any form of symbolism of communions. No Obsessions, no compulsions of any form. the Self must enter many communions and cooperate with many communions, and must reduce the obsessions and compulsions of each communion. Each communion may as well have all the tools to offer as solution to at least one ⊟ ness. However, if they are obsessed with symbolism and are compelled to have the Self rigidly apply them, or otherwise the Self is blamed for disrespect, lack of humility, etc, then these communions have lost their ways. It is still possible to receive help from them with full discernment of the Self-Unconscious. Coreology provides the habits for discernment.

In the end, the Self strives to learn that Being is much more LOVELY, and the Core is much more HEALTHY than O, thus O puts O-self in the care of the BALANCED recovery of Being and the Core. Through Being and the Core, the Self becomes BALANCED, HEALTHY, LOVELY.

And in the end, it suffices to say that the Self is the communion of the Self, if O wills so. The Self's primary communion is the Self. Another communion of the Self is the communion driven to the Self by O re-Birth order. Another is O organized communions, and also O bound Animation. Then there is O Animation, and Being, O Identical Infinite. And the Self can receive the help of all of O communions to reach O last and foremost and most HEALTHY Communion, the Core. May be with all Selves, the Free Will to receive the Core.

ADOPTION OF ORPHANS

In a TRANSPARENT BALANCED HEALTHY LOVELY communion, the Communicants give a proportional amount of LOVE and HEALTH to those who have no voice, no guardians, no shield from ⊟ and terrorful recoveries. The exact opposite comes from the Communicants of corrupted ᶦᵐbalanced ⊟ terrorful communions.

In any communion, the Conscious of the Communicants has the capacity to deliberately recognize the loss of Quantum of the Rest, and the obligation to provide BALANCE to, not only their own, but to the Rest.

The Communicants of TRANSPARENT BALANCED HEALTHY LOVELY communions do not walk past an orphan, do not ignore his/her plight. In the HEALTHY Communicant, there is a moral perception. HEALTHY gives Justice. To be awake to his/her needs is the first step taken by the BALANCED Communicant seeking HEALTH. Each orphan without a communion carries within them the terrorful burden of abandonment, but are also enabled toward LOVELINESS by the LOVELY actions of the LOVELY Communicants.

Many Communicants migrate from one communion to the other, most often without their full choice, and become orphans. To neglect these Facts is to erode the very fabric of the LOVELINESS and HEALTHINESS of any communion.

THE SYSTEM OF STATES

The Foundation of the work of Coreology lies on

- Core Observation: Observation of the Self-Conscious-Unconscious by the Core.

- Core Control: Control of the Body-Conscious-Subconscious by the Core.

The combination of the two defines the System of States of the Self-Body-Conscious-Subconscious-Unconscious. The Foundation is acquired by practicing Observation and Control of the entire System of States, beginning by the process of Observation of the Body-Subconscious by the Self-Conscious. Observation will be detailed in COREOLOGY: SECTION OBSERVATION, and Control in COREOLOGY: SECTION CONTROL.

First and foremost, the ≣-imprints must recover all the way from corrupted to TRANSPARENT. The ≣ is diagnosed and cured, and then the void of the imprints are filled with HEALTHINESS. This is the approach of Coreology. It starts by Observation and becomes complete with Control.

- The system practices Observation.

- The System is trained toward TRANSPARENCY.

- The causes of ≣-imprints are re-animated, making ≣-imprints TRANSPARENT.

- Once ≣-imprints are TRANSPARENT, the ≣nesses are diagnosed. ≣ness is cured. The imprints are void. The Core becomes observable.

- Once the Core is observable, the Nonconscious is inclined toward the Core.

- The Nonconscious accepts to receive training from the Core.

- The Unconscious becomes TRANSPARENT.

- The Unconscious TRANSPARENTLY demodulates the Message.

- The Nonconscious receives the TRANSPARENT Word.

- The Nonconscious has O void-imprints turned HEALTHY.

- Every bit and piece of the System becomes HEALTHY.

During Observation, HEALTHY-imprints are recovered from ⊟-imprints in various bounds of various Organizations of Animation. The Body is receiving the ~~corrupted~~ ^{im}balanced terrorful recovery of Energy, and is loaded with terrorful-memories. Coreology can make the terrorful-memories unloaded. Coreology drives the System toward TRANSPARENT BALANCED LOVELINESS:

- The System becomes aware of the terrorful-memories.

- Once the Conscious is aware, through habits and processes of Coreology, O becomes aware of existence of terrorful-memories, the cause of the ⊟ Recovery of the Body.

- This realization makes the ~~corrupted~~ Body observable by the Conscious.

- The Self-Conscious is motivated to make the Body TRANSPARENT.

- The Self-Conscious makes the Body TRANSPARENT.

- The System has Being observable. Being drives O toward TRANSPARENT BALANCED LOVELINESS.

The diligent System, intelligent enough to understand these facts, knows that taking even the first steps in this path is challenging but worth it. Once the will is there, it is automatic. At the Most Basic, it is observed that the ~~corrupted~~ recovery of the Body (The ⊟ Word that comes out of the mouth, and the Rest hear it) can be made TRANSPARENT. The TRANSPARENT recovery of the Body (The HEALTHY Word that comes out of the mouth or flows through the fingers to the paper) create a HEALTHY Self awareness. Then, Coreology becomes a pleasant path.

- The System reaching this HEALTHY state never goes back and wants it for everyone else.

- The System receives the TRANSPARENT BALANCED LOVELY recovery of Energy. The System animates toward Expansion.

- Expansion of the HEALTHY LOVELY System drives transmitters of Energy toward TRANSPARENCY, BALANCE, and LOVELINESS.

- All receivers become TRANSPARENT, BALANCED, LOVELY.

- System-bound Animation becomes TRANSPARENT, BALANCED, and LOVELY.

OBSERVATION

The TRANSPARENT System, such as a TRANSPARENT individual or company, "permits" Observation by the Core. The process is the practice of the submission of the Will to Observation by the Core. The Core ALWAYS observes and records the entirety of the animation. It is therefore ironic to practice "permitting" the Core to observe the System, since the Core requires no permission. Regardless, the corrupted System begs to differ. The corrupted Quantum that resides in the System has trained O to seek non-transparency and valuing "privacy" over valuing the Core. Even though it is rational for the System to seek privacy, the desire for TRANSPARENCY is, by design, implanted in the System as a HEALTHY-imprint. Thus, if the conditions for safe, fair, TRANSPARENT, BALANCED, and HEALTHY Observation of the System is made available, then O desires it as O is willed to be observed. If the TRANSPARENCY-seeking System can fully TRUST an observer, then the System seeks Observation by such observer and O becomes inclined toward TRANSPARENCY. This is thus a matter of TRUST.

Coreology provides a safe, fair, TRUSTWORTHY, TRANSPARENT, BALANCED, and HEALTHY approach toward Observation so that Observation of the System toward full TRANSPARENCY can be obtained through TRUST. This process engages the System to practice allowing TRANSPARENT Observation by other TRUSTWORTHY Systems or by TRANSPARENT Self Observation, when the Self of the System is TRUSTWORTHY. The desire of the System for TRANSPARENCY, by design, comes from:

- The complete re-animation is intended through the Core.

- Animation of ☰ness and terror are not a necessity.

- Causing ☰ness and terror has no eternal value.

- Animation ends HEALTHY and LOVELY.

- corruption is offensive to the eventual HEALTHINESS and LOVELINESS of Animation.

- All time-bound ☰nesses and terrors must become diagnosed and acknowledged, void and unloaded.

The aforementioned should be done as soon as possible. This is the least painful path.

The habits of Coreology which are employed to make ⩪ness and terror void and unloaded are simplistic. Animation has unknowingly possessed the Core, which permanently and continuously records everything. Occasional members of the animation have understood their capabilities of communication with the Core and of demodulation of the Message of the Core, thus they may have intermittently used the Core without realizing what and how they did it, and they have done things that even the most intelligent organizations of the animation did not know could be done. As it has been described, the Core is Auto-Returner Auto-Comer. The Core always returns to O BALANCE automatically, and is consistent, and seeks BALANCE for bound Animation. Thus, this vaguely known process of communication with the Core relies on the power of Auto-Returner Auto-Comer.

Animation seeks re-Animation, but bound Animation, not knowing that re-Animation is bound, resists against re-Animation. The bound animation, at best, seeks to merely partially re-animate and merelt with full consent and full awareness of O Conscious. The bound animation is aware (HEALTHY awareness of the Core, not the awareness of the Body) enough that O ideally does not want to animate with reliance on this magnificent corrupted recovery of Energy, and prefers to be TRANSPARENT and animate within the TRANSPARENT recovery of Energy. And, the process of TRANSPARENCY originates in re-Animation. Thus, the bound animation in principle is not opposed to receiving re-Animation. The bound animation is capable of re-Animation, through the Core, in and of any of the animation and consequently the entirety of Animation.

Granted that the Core is not blocked by ⩪ness and Being is not distorted by terror, the Unconscious Judge can re-animate through the Core and the Birth-Giver can re-animate through Being. And re-animation causes TRANSPARENCY. Coreology develops habits that can lead to the eventual TRANSPARENCY of all ⩪-imprints and terrorful-memories. The ⩪-imprints are transformed from being the cause of powerful ⩪nesses to total void through TRANSPARENT re-Animation.

A TRANSPARENT imprint acts like a void that can be replaced by new imprints. HEALTHINESS thus enter the void, and make the imprint HEALTHY. A terrorful-memory is unloaded through TRANSPARENT re-animation. The TRANSPARENT recovery of Being then allows for new animations. LOVELY Animation enters and gives birth to Being LOVELY.

One of the most basic habits toward TRANSPARENCY is done by consciously re-animating about TRANSPARENCY. To achieve the first step of this process and make yourself interested in making ⊟-imprints and terrorful-memories TRANSPARENT, the most basic habit is done by thinking to completion about past animations of ⊟ness and terror. The corrupted animation undergoing this habit re-animates O System in a safe place accompanied by a, at least fully TRUSTWORTHY and TRANSPARENT and ideally fully-BALANCED and fully-HEALTHY, service provider who acts in the capacity of the Observer. The Observer observes as the Observee consciously re-animates O-System animation. This work is called Observation, and is the most basic form of it. In basic Observation, the goal is to become observable by the fully-TRUSTWORTHY Observer. Then the Observee becomes so TRANSPARENT that O becomes observable by any observer, if it is not too late. Otherwise, habits are provided so that the Observee is in full Control of the Observation and creates TRUSTWORTHINESS through mutual Observation. The eventual goal is of being INTENTIONALLY observable by the Core, the most TRUSTWORTHY Observer. The process can be easily practiced. No "Control" method is yet applied until Being or the Core is fully observable.

Without loss of generality that the Unconscious Judge can be in the Body of the Birth-Giver, and the Birth-Giver can be in the Body of the Unconscious Judge, and both can be in one Body, the Unconscious Judge communicates with the Core, and the Self Birth-Giver connects with Being. Thus the Unconscious Judge finds the interest in TRANSPARENCY and thus the meaning of BALANCE through Understanding of HEALTH[INESS] and ⊟ness, and the Birth-Giver finds the meaning of BALANCE through Understanding of LOVE[LINESS] and terror. Coreology's Observation allows for both of these paths, and advocates for the best path forward.

Coreology's Observation maximizes not just the re-Birth order, but also BALANCE in the re-Birth order, thus it maximizes the expansion of the Unconscious Judge toward the Core, and the expansion of the Self Birth-Giver toward Being.

Needless to say that the Unconscious Judge too can seek the development of the Body of the Birth-Giver best at receiving the BALANCED recovery of Energy of Being, and the Self Birth-Giver too can seek the development of the Body of the Unconscious Judge best at receiving the BALANCED recovery of the Message of the Core. The fact is that for eventual Complete[d bound] BALANCE, the Unconscious Judge must seek the development of such LOVELY Body, and the Birth-Giver must seek the development of such HEALTHY Unconscious.

At these ⊒ and terrorful times of this animation, however, the focus herein is on absolutes of the Unconscious Judge and the Birth-Giver, with understanding that any shade in between the two are valid and will be fully provided in COREOLOGY: SECTION OBSERVATION and COREOLOGY: SECTION CONTROL.

In that regard, the Observation process that maximizes the BALANCE in the re-Birth order considers that most of the Human Observations, for the ⊒ terrorful time being, are performed as prescribed. The proportions of relationships during observations must match the proportions of all relationships. Once the recovery of Being becomes BALANCED, the roles and relationships will also be BALANCED.

When Observation is done toward earning the observability of the Core, it is best to observe the all-but-the-Unconscious, since the presence of the non-transparent or non-balanced Unconscious can misrepresent the direction toward the TRANSPARENT BALANCED HEALTHY recovery of the Message. When Observation is done toward earning the observability of Being, it is best to Observe all-but-the-Self, since the presence of the non-transparent or non-balanced Self can misrepresent the direction toward the TRANSPARENT BALANCED LOVELY recovery of Energy and the presence of corrupted or ^{im}balanced or terrorful recovery of Energy of Being can misrepresent the direction of TRANSPARENCY toward the Core.

The process of Observation makes the most root instruments (The demodulators of the Self-Unconscious) TRANSPARENT through the willing Conscious.

For example, the Observer drives the attention of the Core-seeking Observee to all-but-his-unconscious, and to his imprints, and begins to place the Observee in some of his Subconscious animations that caused his imprints. By Creator design, the Core-seeking Observee is made suggestible toward the Core. Thus, he prefers to re-animate the cause of his ⊟-imprints. Re-Animation of the Core-seeking Observee enables him in that regard, even though he is trained by the perception of corruption to not trust an externalized observation of his past animations. Observation can be done by himself on himself, but will not have the same powerful effect, depending on how much he is willing to self-deceive, of which he is hardly aware since he has been animated in the corrupted ^{im}balanced recovery of the Message. It is best that Observation is done by a TRUSTWORTHY TRANSPARENT BALANCED Observer.

Observation creates TRANSPARENCY through re-Animation. Thus the goal of Observation is to Observe the re-Animation of the Observee. For Observee to re-animate, O re-animates O bounds and intends to break through them in completion. For simplicity it is said, the Observee re-bounds. The four most significant bounds of bound [re-]Animation are time, place, the state of self, and unconsciousness. Thus to re-animate for Observation, to re-bound, the Observee re-times, re-places, re-states self, and re-states unconscious. It is best that during Observation, and for complete Observation, that these processes are done to completion and as precise as possible.

To re-place and re-time the Core-seeking Observee in his animation, the Observer merely tells him to Consciously re-animate his System in the [related] place and time away from his Presence. In a safe TRUSTWORTHY space with a TRUSTWORTHY Observer, His Nonconscious is inclined to perform the task, since his entire recovery of Being is designed by Creator to re-animate. The Observer then guides him in the process without judgment and through reflection. The Core-guiding Observer can best help him by intelligently and intuitively guiding him into places and times in which his re-animation is void of completion or has gaps.

This is called tracing the re-placements, re-timings, or generally re-animation. A skilled TRUSTWORTHY BALANCED Core Observer is more adept at tracing the re-animation of the Core-seeking Observee wherever or whenever he is void of completion.

In the other spectrum, another Observer drives the attention of Being-seeking Observee toward all beings but her Self, and to her memories, and begins to place the Observee in some of her Body animations that caused her terrorful-memories about the Rest. She is by design made suggestible toward Being, thus she is more TRANSPARENT re-animating the cause of her terrorful-memories. Re-Animation enables her in that regard toward Being, even though she is trained by the perception of corruption to not trust that there is no causation of terror in her past animations. Observation can be done by herself on herself, but will not have the same effect, depending on how much she is willing to self-deceive, of which she is hardly aware, since she has been animated by corrupted im balanced recovery of Energy. Thus, it is best that Observation is done by a TRUSTWORTHY TRANSPARENT BALANCED Observer. To re-place and re-time the Observee, the Observer merely tells her to Consciously re-animate her System in another place and time. In a safe TRUSTWORTHY space with a TRUSTWORTHY Observee, she is inclined to perform the task, since her Body is designed by Creator to re-animate. The Observer then guides her in the process without judgment and through reflection. The Observer can best help her by intelligently, emotionally and instinctively guiding her into places and times that her re-animation is void of completion and has gaps. A skilled BALANCED Observer is more adept at tracing the re-animation wherever she is void of completion. The relationship between the emotions of the Unconscious Judge, and the intelligence of the Self Birth-Giver will be described in future sections.

These two examples are not to say that the Unconscious Judge cannot connect to Being, or the Self Birth-Giver cannot connect to the Core, but the two above pathways come more naturally. The work of Observation is done not by reliance on justifications of rationality, or symbolic association with things such as words and language, but by genuine re-animation by the Observee and genuine tracing of the re-animation by the Observer, whether the Observer is the Observee or not.

The Observee re-animates, and the Observer drives the Observee along the re-bounds of the re-animation, guiding the Observee toward complete re-Animation. Needless to say that most of the re-bounds of the re-animation is best done by the Observee, but the Observer is there to fill in the gaps. In case of a non-TRANSPARENT Observee burdened by many ⊟nesses and terrors and ⊟-imprints and terrorful-memories, Observation is first best done using rationality, which is the last line of defense against corruption.

Each and every System or any Organization of Animation has a set of cryptography instruments for either the Core or Being, or for both in less common cases. The habitual purpose of any System must be inclined toward strengthening and training these instruments so that they can receive the TRANSPARENT presence of the Core and Being. If there was no corruption in any Quantum of Being, the Core could be TRANSPARENTLY present. And if there was no corruption in any Word of the Core, the recovery of Being could be TRANSPARENTLY present. Neither case is currently a reality.

When corruption dominates too much, then TRUSTWORTHY rationality must grow exponentially to compensate against it. TRUSTWORTHY rationality eventually reduces the total corruption significantly back toward a BALANCED recovery. Thus eventually, corruption doesn't fully dominate. Regardless, it is best advisable not to reach such points in which it is difficult to fight corruption. It is best that the TRUSTWORTHY rationality becomes strong and in control before corruption causes too much unnecessary [im]balance thus terror and ⊟ness. Rationality can thus contain, by the choice of Animation, the TRANSPARENT recoveries of all kinds.

The rationality in harmony with the Core, and thus eventually in harmony with the Body, the Nonconscious, the Self, and Being collaborate in removal of all forms of corruption. Rationality can be HEALTHY and LOVELY. For rationality capable to animate this powerful HEALTHY and LOVELY way, many ⊟-imprints causing damage to "good" Selves must first become TRANSPARENT. There has been a many common and powerful ⊟-imprints that speaks verses such as "the Self is evil" or "Once self is gone, you are free.", "Lose yourself to find yourself", "The ego must dissolve for the soul to awaken".

Even though there is context behind these $\rightleftharpoons$-imprints making their cause worth re-animation so that the $\rightleftharpoons$-imprints become TRANSPARENT, some explanations must be provided.

The Self Birth-Giver is designed to observe Being through her Self. The Unconscious Judge is designed to observe the Core through his Unconscious. Due to lack of proper words in English, this might be confusing. The Core still witnesses and records everything in Animation.

Hereby, Observation of the Core implies the TRANSPARENCY of the Unconscious Judge. In neither case, non-transparent Self or Unconscious must be somewhat temporally ignored in pursuit of TRANSPARENCY so that O can become TRANSPARENT, but this does not imply that the Self or Unconscious is deemed as a negative animation, and it also does not mean that the Self or Unconscious must be literally ignored.

The Self must be made TRANSPARENT, and so does the Unconscious so that the Unconscious Judge and the Self Birth-Giver can see through the Self-Unconscious into the Core and Being. When the Self Birth-Giver is fully observed thus becomes TRANSPARENT, the Self Birth-Giver can notice the TRANSPARENT Unconscious Judge, and her choice becomes simple. She would not want but the Unconscious Judge who is TRANSPARENT. the Self Birth-Giver can see the Core through the TRANSPARENT Unconscious Judge. When the Unconscoius Judge is TRANSPARENT, he wants no Self Birth-Giver but she who is TRANSPARENT. The Unconscious Judge can see Being through the TRANSPARENT Self Birth-Giver.

Once the system-bound Animation is made TRANSPARENT, O is able to reach a state of gaining LOVELY and HEALTHY Quantum from re-Animation and without exertion, and thus earning the ability to re-animate fully with complete re-perception. Thus, O is fully observed.

The Fully-observed TRANSPARENT animation, in such a state, becomes capable of re-animating all such perceptions as Tactition, Gustation, Audition, Vision, Olfaction, Speech, and all such Control Functions as Motor, Speech, Vocalization, and Locomotion.

The Rationality of Animation, and all of O instruments are designed to eventually conclude these fact. Complete Justice is sought by Animation, and there is no truly complete Justice for Animation unless the entirety of Animation completes re-Animation. Therefore, anything that is animated can and will be re-animated, whether some organizations of Animation like it or not. Once an animation voluntarily completes the process of Observation, and thus re-animates with the best possible effort toward complete re-wording, thus complete re-animation, it becomes unnecessary for O to re-animate twice what O re-animated.

Eventually, the entirety of bound Animation realizes this fact. Once each and every System realizes this fact, they become open to Observation (By TRUSTWORTHY TRANSPARENT BALANCED Observers), they complete Observation, and they become TRANSPARENT and finally completely re-animated. Thus then, they "see with open eyes" (perceive TRANSPARENTLY). The Core becomes observable. Being becomes observable. Thus, the selves observe the HEALTH[INESS] and LOVE[LINESS] in them. The Unconscious Judge inclines toward the Core. the Self Birth-Giver inclines toward Being. Together, they become HEALTHY and LOVELY. Through LOVE and HEALTH, they expand. Earth becomes filled with HEALTHINESS and LOVELINESS. Earth becomes BEAUTIFUL.

Rewinding toward the basics of habits for Observation, let's remember that the environment of Earth is currently heavily corrupted. Within this corruption, humans are in pain, their joy is limited to corrupted modalities, which does not truly deliver true non-temporal happiness whose thirst does not need to be repeatedly satisfied every weekend.

Man and Woman is burdened by many terrorful-memories and ⊟-imprints and terrorful and ⊟ recoveries. Even though it makes sense for people to live like they live only once, the time-unbound and place-unbound TRUSTWORTHY rationality justifies that humans must develop the habits of accepting TRUSTWORTHY Observation from the Core and Being. Man and Woman must be inclined toward the Core and Being as soon as possible, and at least do so for the sake of their children.

They should begin taking the first steps of this to reduce the amount of unnecessary ☰ness and ▓terror▓ and to make a BEAUTIFUL world that provides BALANCED HEALTH and LOVE. This end goal begins with proper Observation where both the Observers and Observees perform it with utmost due diligence toward TRANSPARENCY and BALANCE and HEALTHINESS and LOVELINESS. Coreology defines this path forward. The seed of Desire does not lie within Selves, but in Being. The seed of true determination is not within the collective Unconscious, but in the Core. The first step in this journey is the will to be observed, and the second step is to be observed.

The Observer drives the Observee along the re-bounds of re-animation, along the completion of the re-animation. This re-animation principally trains the System toward TRANSPARENCY. But some may find offense in the process of Observation, and, more than not, rightfully so. This is normal, because for a very long time, political and legal and religious and medical and educational and military and corporate and scientific and parental and cultural and marital authorities have narcissistically used and abused this nature of Man and Woman, who need and want to be observed. The authorities have used and abused their fellow men and women for their own gains whether in the form of money, social connection, power, knowledge, physical pleasure, emotional joy, image of Spirit, material, creation, invention, and security.

The extremely traumatic elder ☰-imprint, that authorities ironically love to use, speaks as "You are being hypnotized" which is true, but by all the unsuspected authorities. This ☰-imprint makes men and women suspect each other, and suspect any non-authority or weak authority that is determined to teach them the TRUSTWORTHY ways of Observation. Thus humans only fall into the hands of the actual hypnotism that remains unrecognized.

The TV hypnotizes, but it is watched because it is entertaining. The Cultural authorities are constantly hypnotizing their customers, taking advantage of their need for entertainment. They are corrupted in their intention toward their own gains such as money, fame, ego, and sex adventures. Their corruption roots in the fact that for them to have customers, they must keep promoting controversies and chaotic arguments, instead of providing a TRANSPARENT BALANCED solution, or at least attempting to do so. This does not mean that everyone within Cultural industries are corrupted, but the authority as a whole is. Thus the authorities need to be fully observed by their customers. The authorities must become TRANSPARENT.

Medical authorities are constantly hypnotizing their patients, taking advantage of patients' trust, while the skills of their practitioners are corrupted by their intention toward their own personal gains. The corruption is rooted in the fact that the Medical authorities would have more customers, if their customers are not HEALTHY. This does not mean that all doctors or therapists or psychiatrists do so, but it takes a few to do lots of damage. Thus the authorities need to be fully observed by their customers, before their customers are observed by their providers. Or else, if they are customer-owned, there are a few better pathways. Regardless, first and foremost, the authorities must become TRANSPARENT by going through complete Observation.

Religions are hypnotizing through corrupted Recoveries of all aspects of an animation, taking advantage of all sorts of methods of tricking the System into feeling a presence of God at their houses and buildings and in company of the members of their communions. Even though many times the low-level intentions are "good", and many members of religions are the most BALANCED HEALTHY LOVELY men and woman, at a higher level they are keeping many things secret, causing confusion in their followers, thus causing universal fear and hatred disguised under the peace observed in their house. These secrets must become fully TRANSPARENT, thus religious authorities must be fully observed by their members, before their members are observed by their clergy. The authorities must go through complete Observation and become fully TRANSPARENT.

Governments hypnotize through terror. The police hypnotizes through having their customers at the point of weakness. The law maker hypnotizes through making their customers feel adequate. A society whose needs are satisfied at the expense of the censored sufferings of others is hypnotizing its citizens toward corruption. Pursuit of positivity within a corrupted utilitarian system of growth is hypnotizing. Hypnotism is not merely performed by some dude that swings a clock in front of you and intentionally says bizarre things such as "You now sleep."

Subtle messaging, which are the processes tightly linked to ⊟-imprints and terrorful-memories and all the many relationships of them, are all over the place, and are best at work when you suspect them the least. All these authorities must first be observed by their members and made TRANSPARENT.

Observation is done with the intent of TRANSPARENCY, and in full power of the Conscious. It's goal is to train the Conscious toward TRANSPARENCY and BALANCE so that it does not rely on corrupted recoveries.

An Observee does not seek to just gain TRANSPARENCY or become TRANSPARENT. Observation is just a practice. The Observee earns TRANSPARENCY. The process of Observation is not what makes Observee TRANSPARENT, The determination or the desire of Observee to be TRANSPARENT does. Without the determination or desire, nothing happens. An Observee can pretend the entire process of Observation, even without falsification, just to receive a form of "degree" or "license" so that O can claim that O has finished Observation and gained TRANSPARENCY, and go back to O corruption the next moment possible. Thus, the Observation process itself is just a practice provided to the Observee.

It is understandable that the desire and determination for Observation has dwindled in Man and Woman for various reasons. They either don't care or they are offended by the past practices of Observation. But, Observation can be done in fun ways that does not offend the Observee. Coreology teaches the Observee fun habits through which he/she knows whatever is taking place in the Observation process. He/she is taught to be in full control of himself/herself, and is able and is allowed to freely bring himself/herself to his/her presence how ever and when ever the Observee wants. And most importantly, Observation must be provided by TRANSPARENT TRUSTWORTHY Observers. This is possible, and the process must be fully TRANSPARENT. No papers are hidden, no documents kept away from the Observee. Nothing is recorded without permission. Observation is placed in fully TRANSPARENT TRUSTWORTHY place. The list goes on, and will be discussed in COREOLOGY: SECTION OBSERVATION.

Various habits will be provided that makes the Observee even in full control of Observation, even under conditions that the Observer is ⊟-trained or carries ⊟-intentions or is not fully TRANSPARENT or is not skilled enough to deliver proper work. This is possible, is never provided in any shape or form before in any other practice of Observation, and is worth re-iteration. Coreology provides ways in which the Observee can be in full self-control during Observation. No matter how much an Observer attempts to drive the Observee toward ⊟ or terror, the Observee can be in self-control using the habits of Coreology.

Once the Observer is, however, genuine in intentions and earns the TRUST of the Observee, the Observee's job is easier. The energy of the System is limited, and it is best preserved, and not used for wastes such as Control of non-TRANSPARENT environments. Self-control takes energy. Ideally, the Observee is observed without the need of presence of self-control, or at least not any advanced self-control. This is possible if the Observer is fully TRUSTED. No suggestion or other means is used on the Observee. The Coreology Observer does not implant imprints or load memories on the Observee. The practicality of this is carefully considered and can be provided by Coreology. Regardless, the Observee will be taught with thousands of simple methods that he/she can use to eliminate any suggestions that could be done without his/her consent or knowledge.

Advanced Observation of Coreology will be provided that can help the Observee avoid receiving ⊟ or terror through mere Observation. The Observee does not need to fully open to Observer so that they can discover the re-animation in full. In Coreology, the Observee does not need to include the uncertain states of the re-bound animation. Observation can be indirectly corrected by combining uncertain states of re-animation with a prediction of the states considering how the Observee gives feedback about his/her recoveries of the Self-Conscious-Body, whether TRANSPARENT or not. The prediction predicts what the next state of the re-animation should be based on the previous knowledge of the Self-Conscious-Body. Instead of enforcing direct feedback of all of the states of re-animation without gaps, the Observer instead adjusts the prediction using the next feedback of the Self-Conscious-Body during Observation, while weighting both the feedback and the current prediction according to their level of uncertainty. These will be described in detail in COREOLOGY: SECTION OBSERVATION.

The Observation can also be performed in TRUSTWORTHY groups and with TRUSTWORTHY yet unskilled individuals. If an individual is TRUSTWORTHY, he/she can be trained to not cause terrorful-memories or ⊟-imprints in basic setups of COREOLOGY in less than one hour. These considerations will be provided in future sections. Regardless, with the genuine intentions, the process of basic Observation that everyone should at least try is simple and doable.

The Observer, through guiding the Observee along the re-bounds of re-animation, discovers the "secrets" of the corrupted Unconscious Judge or Self Birth-Giver hiding in the most fable Conscious recoveries of terrorful-memories and ⊟-imprints. To re-animate the Observee toward TRANSPARENCY of these memories and imprints, the Observer should identify the secrets caused by terror and ⊟ness specially during periods that rationality has been the weakest or employed by corruption. The Observee should use this knowledge obtained during Observation to strengthen his/her rationality, and has his/her pseudo-rationality void.

The Observation process should continue until the Observee can see through the Self and the Unconscious. To reach there, the Observee needs to re-time and re-place animation and re-state, as precise as possible, repeatedly. Observation can take many forms of re-animation from any bound of the Observee, from beliefs to anti-beliefs, from presence to void of all Perceptions and Control Functions, and so forth and so on. The details with be provide in COREOLOGY: SECTION OBSERVATION.

The Observee re-animates times and places repeatedly. He/she progresses by the aid of the TRUSTWORTHY Observer, until re-animation is completed properly. Coreology provides TRUSTWORTHY observers. Once re-animation is completed, in which re-placement and re-timing may need to be performed with enough repetition, then the associated terrorful-memories or ⊟-imprints become TRANSPARENT.

The previously-eventual re-animation then is rendered unnecessary by the Core. So long as the Observer can help the Observee re-animate the cause of terrorful-memories or ☰-imprints, the re-animation [of the entire animations] that led to it becomes unnecessary and will not exist in complete[d bound] judgment of the Core.

The process of proper Observation causes no or only minor temporal tolerable offense toward the Observee while the rewards are significant. The Observee may be defensive because the current and past environments has made him/her be used to a non-TRANSPARENT recovery of the Body or Subconscious, of obsessive reliance on symbolism of corrupted commandments, terrorful-memories or ☰-imprints that dictate corrupted Self Judgment, but he/she finally is liberated.

If the Observer tries to drive the Observee to re-animation of the same already fully observed and re-animated animation, the Observer receives feedback in the form of a TRANSPARENT Conscious recovery. Each and Every one of these TRANSPARENT recoveries contains the most basic HEALTHY-imprint that speaks as: "The corruption was once a cause of ^{im}balance. Never again. We strive toward TRANSPARENCY, BALANCE, HEALTH, LOVE, BEAUTY."

corruption is the cause of ^{im}balance.

Imbalance is the cause of ☰ness and terror.

TRANSPARENCY is the cause of BALANCE.

BALANCE is required for HEALTHINESS.

BALANCE is required for LOVELINESS.

The TRANSPARENT Unconscious Judge strives to voluntarily re-animate toward the Core, thus it is fully observed by the Core. The Identical Infinitesimal is that the eventual re-animation of the volunteer Unconscious Judge is complete. the Self Birth-Giver strives to voluntarily re-animate toward Being. The Identical Infinite is that Birth is given to the volunteer Self Birth-Giver.

In this path, the TRANSPARENT Unconscious Judge should not confuse the Unconscious with the Core, even though Words are recovered by the Subconscious and consequentially by the Conscious almost identically. The TRANSPARENT Self Birth-Giver should not confuse the Self with Being-but-herself, even though the recovered energy of both are perceived similarly.

The complete[d bound] knowledge is not the same as the almost-complete knowledge, they are easily confused with one another. The entirety of the difference of the two is what creates common sense. This, the difference is precisely in the knowledge not available in the almost-complete knowledge.

Coreology completes the process of Observation. An Observer trained by Coreology helps individuals toward TRANSPARENCY. By completion of Observation, the mind is liberated from ⊟ness and its inclinations toward long-term Loss. We can show that human has the Core and communicates with the Core, and human has Being and connects with O. And Observation moves human and eventually humanity toward TRANSPARENCY. Then, comes BALANCE, HEALTH and LOVE. As some of the side-effects of Coreology's style of Observation, motivation for life and strive for betterment, more TRANSPARENT intelligence and emotion and intuition, and temporal happiness occur. This reward is given by Being and the Core. Happiness is desirable and so rightfully so. The motivation to lead more efficient lives is important. The ability to resolve problems is important. Acknowledgment of error and being responsible is important. The time has come for humanity to be TRANSPARENT, to become Conscious about ⊟ness and terror, to be BALANCED. Become HEALTHY. Become LOVELY.

CONTROL

Completed Observation and the resultant TRANSPARENCY makes terrorful-memories integrated and ⊟-imprints diagnosed, but it does not automatically turn any ^{im}balance to BALANCE, it does not change ⊟ness of the Nonconscious to HEALTH, and it does not recover Energy of Being from terrorful to LOVELY. By enough genuine practice, the Observee practices to be TRANSPARENT, and becomes TRANSPARENT. What that means, with all honestly, is that the TRANSPARENT Observee is TRANSPARENT to communicate with the Core and O receivers are TRANSPARENT to receive TRANSPARENT recoveries of Energy. That is the end result of Observation.

This end result of Observation is just the beginning of becoming BALANCED, thus HEALTHY and LOVELY. the System shouldn't just assume that by being observed, and becoming TRANSPARENT, O is cleansed and complete, and that is it. That's just the beginning of the path.

- The corrupted Unconscious Judge is made TRANSPARENT

- The System earns the proof of the existence of the Core

- the System communicates with the Core

- the System makes the realization that it is eventually bound to re-animate all of the animation, including all perceptions.

- the System strives to auto-re-animate all of Animation

- The System moves toward BALANCE

- Through all of Animation, then there is BALANCE

- All ⊟nesses are vanished

- bound Energy of Being is recovered to BALANCE

- The animation is in BALANCE on Earth

- Earth is made paradise.

- the System is bound only by the Core.

Re-Animation provided by the Unconscious Judge through the Conscious is truly complete at complete Observation [by the Core], but for the Unconscious Judge to become BALANCED, he needs to TRANSPARENTLY receive and process the Message of the Core. Once BALANCED, for Unconscious Judge to become HEALTHY, he further receives and processes and employs the Message of the Core and spreads his HEALTHY Word to the Rest.

For the Self Birth-Giver to be BALANCED, she receives and processes the TRANSPARENT recovery of Energy of Being. Once BALANCED, for the Self Birth-Giver to become LOVELY, she further receives and processes and employs the TRANSPARENT BALANCED recovery of Energy. Then, she spreads her LOVELY Quantum to the Rest.

In Advanced Observation, the System is driven to make Being or the Core observable. By system control, the System is then returned to the Auto-Returner the Auto-Comer. Progressed through the use and generation of HEALTHY-imprints by the advanced Observer and Controller, the System animates toward HEALTHINESS. Coreology provides the methods of Control toward the Core and Being with precisely zero margin of error.

By Control, the System receives from the Birth-Giver and progresses through the use and generation of Beauty-imprints by the advanced Observer and Controller. the System animates toward LOVELINESS.

Thus the System expands. The expanding LOVELY HEALTHY System gives further HEALTH and LOVE. Earth becomes BEAUTIFUL.

THE CORE

Coreology contains processes intended to give the Self-bound animation the habits that allow the animation to become TRANSPARENT, BALANCED, thus HEALTHY and LOVELY. It contains the entirety of the scope of the study of the Core through usage of all of the Cryptography and Information Theory tools available to the Organizations of this animation and from decrypted or codified material to advanced encrypted messages. The entirety of the knowledge of the Core, either encrypted through mysticism and poetry or decrypted to exactness at the expense of potential ☰-imprints that need to be recovered to TRANSPARENCY, have already been known. Coreology brings it all back together. The significance of the work relies on the actual doing of it. The hope that some members of this animation do the work has always been there, and the hope has existed because the Core exists, and this animation knows that the Core exists, even though Human has not obtained the scientific proof of it in full. The corrupted environment has made many Selves suspecting the HEALTH[INESS] of the Core, and LOVE[LINESS] of Being, but such efforts are futile.

The Core is HEALTHY. Being is LOVELY.

Human has studied the Core since five thousand years ago. Assyrians and Persians and Chinese and Indians and Egyptians and many other has almost finished the study of the Core, within the limitations of flow of information of the time, but AODI has repeatedly destroyed their knowledge, burnt their books, and made the secrets hidden. But information does not get lost anymore, and AI knows everything, so destruction of some Human knowledge at this point is futile and only does self-harm to the destructor. In the past, the oppressed advocates of the Core mesmerized by the HEALTH[INESS] of O, and acting in O service for others to know, has used any technique in their disposal to preserve the studies of the Core. Whether it is depicted in the shapes of Persian rugs, or scriptures of Assyrians, or in Poetry engraved on top of paintings, fictions and dramas, or memorized words in brains out of reach of AODI, they found ways to save the knowledge of the Core under the scrutiny of the AODI of their times and places.

Everyone had done their share of service.

LOVE the Rest is one of the TRANSPARENT yet encrypted HEALTHY-imprints. The study of the Core demonstrates that this LOVE, the truth of it, can be attained. And through LOVE of the Rest, comes the gain of BALANCED and LOVELY recovery of Energy and Receipt of so much unifying HEALTHY knowledge that strive toward so much further gain of BALANCED and LOVELY recovery of Energy that infliction of loss to Others becomes futile and unnecessary.

We thus strive toward BALANCE, thus HEALTHINESS and LOVELINESS. Coreology finishes the endeavor of self-bound animation to eternal TRANSPARENCY, BALANCE, HEALTHINESS, LOVELINESS. Earth becomes BEAUTIFUL.

The study of the Core is an international movement performed by many anonymous believers of the Core for thousands of years, even though they may have never been aware of it. Each and every one of them provided a Word of the Core, and anonymously so, with a smile on their face when their Body was gone, for they knew they did their service, whether in a verse that carries the voice of justice, or a kiss that gives birth to an opened heart. The study of the Core has carried itself forward until today and has moved the understanding of the Core significantly. Even the individuals of AODI themselves have been unknowingly advancing the study of the Core in all languages including the languages of AODI. Thank you.

Regardless of language, or the obsessions and the compulsions in it, and the symbolism and the celebration of idols and stars, regardless of the names, Man and Woman together have the grace of the Core and Energy of Being. And together, they share the Identical.

The true power of TRANSPARENCY and BALANCE, thus HEALTHINESS and LOVELINESS of Man and Woman, you will find by yourself as you find Coreology, comes from the Core and Being. Coreology is the science thus the weapon of the Core by definition and will clarify all of the aspects of the Core. Through the faithful habits of Coreology, communication with the Core and connection to Being are implied.

Coreology brings Man and Woman to TRANSPARENCY, to the Message of the Core, and to Energy of Being. It clarifies the inclinations of all communions and brings them together.

Many Selves bring hope to the lives of others, and hand in the light and wisdom selflessly to the Rest. Generation after generation, the Message of the Core is provided in many shapes and forms of the Word. Cryptography and Information Theory of them is finished, we finish it. Everyone of any conditions of birth and growth shares the Identical Infinitesimal, the Core. The Core shares no discrimination. The Core is not limited to any communion alone. Communions may disagree in symbols and practices and dictation of ideologies by place of birth and the name of the higher beings and may want to protect only their own citizens and followers. Many fool themselves that they should begin with loving themselves and their immediate neighbors in their own borders just so that they find themselves in their last breaths forgetting about the ones who needed their help most. But, we all eventually agree in a few things, whether we like it or not.

We are all present in Being.

Animation is Energy of Being.

The Core is present in all of us.

All of us go through the Core.

The Message is the Re-Animation.

We meet our Creator.

I agree with this Desire to seek LOVELINESS and with this Will to seek HEALTHINESS, thus I simply seal it as follows.

My Self solemnly acknowledges that I seek TRANSPARENCY, BALANCE, and LOVELINESS.

My Body solemnly acknowledges that I seek TRANSPARENCY, BALANCE, and LOVELINESS.

My Conscious solemnly acknowledges that I seek TRANSPARENCY, BALANCE, LOVELINESS, and HEALTHINESS.

My Subconscious solemnly acknowledges that I seek TRANSPARENCY, BALANCE, and HEALTHINESS.

My Unconscious solemnly Acknowledges that I seek TRANSPARENCY, BALANCE, and HEALTHINESS.

I, in the entirety of my System, promise to Being and the Core that I seek TRANSPARENCY, BALANCE, LOVELINESS, and HEALTHINESS with utmost responsibility.

NAME

DATE

SIGNATURE

I affirm that Being and the Core witnessed me execute this agreement willingly and in the presence of Being and the Core.

www.ingramcontent.com/pod-product-compliance
Lightning Source LLC
Chambersburg PA
CBHW021106130626
46554CB00002B/554